# Giving Spirit a Voice

## The mechanics of mediumship

Ioanna Serpanos

**Ioanna Serpanos**
**Melbourne, Victoria**
**www.ioannaserpanos.com**

Publisher's Note: Some names in this book have been changed to protect the identity of the person.
The information, views, opinions and visuals expressed in this publication are solely those of the author and publisher. The author and publisher disclaims any liabilities or responsibilities whatsoever for any damages, libel or liabilities arising directly or indirectly from the contents of this publication.

Book Layout © 2017 BookDesignTemplates.com
Book Cover © 2019 Bladecreative.com.au
Editor: Frances Key theteambooks.com
Editor: Tricia Dearborn uwap.uwa.edu.au/products/Autobiochemistry

**Giving Spirit A Voice/ Ioanna Serpanos**. -- 1st ed.
ISBN-13: 978-0-6485250-0-4 (hard cover)
ISBN-13: 978-0-6485250-1-1 (paperback)

To my beloved Christine,
for giving me, *a party in my heart*.
To G and all my spirit helpers, teachers and inspirers,
thank you from the bottom of my heart.
To Mavis Pitilla, thank you for your inspirational teachings
and for igniting my soul.

# CONTENTS

# Introduction

> *'Our chief want is someone who will inspire us to be what we know we could be.'*
>
> ~ *Ralph Waldo Emerson*

If you've picked up this book, chances are that you or someone you know has had some experience with Spirit. You are possibly curious to find out more about your own nature and skills, and to understand how this process of contact and communication actually works. You might also be interested in healing and helping others who are going through the grieving process, a process that is inevitably experienced by everyone. Or, quite simply, you might have been drawn to this book and not know exactly why – yet.

*So ... what is a medium?* In the simplest of terms, a medium is a channel of communication between two worlds: the world of Spirit and the world of humanity. The aim of a medium is to demonstrate that life is eternal. This aim is achieved when the medium provides *evidential information* as proof of survival.

A medium's messages to a sitter (the one who is receiving the reading) are considered to be evidential when they contain accurate facts and meaningful nuances that the medium could not know by any other means. A quality medium strives to bring forward the personality of the Spirit person, often expressing mannerisms and characteristics that categorically demonstrate to the sitter that the one communicating is in fact their loved one.

Mediumship may be considered a call to service. The medium is there to serve the Spirit world, not the other way around. I'm not implying that mediums are subservient to Spirit; rather, they stand before Spirit, creating a circle of energy through which Spirit speaks. The medium's priority is to offer their skills to Spirit for the purposes of spiritual communication and healing. Additionally, they give support to the client, holding space and bearing witness to things that had been left unsaid, hurts that had been unresolved, forgiveness granted, joys recalled and gratitude expressed. They do this not only for the client seeking a reading but also for Spirit, whose intent is always to facilitate healing.

Through understanding this healing aspect of the work, the way of approaching Spirit becomes more respectful and the connection deepens as a result. We move beyond the superficial evidence and reach to the core of why the Spirit person has appeared. We understand and bring forth the main reason they've made contact – so that healing can occur.

Mediumship ability occurs in all walks of life and is not restricted to spiritually inclined people. I graduated with a Bachelor of Engineering and worked as a professional engineer for twelve years before I acknowledged my calling and abilities.

It is not unusual for new mediums to initially be unaware of their abilities. They may uncover their ability through a challenging situation such as a life-threatening illness, a near-death-experience (NDE), or an accident, for example. Other times, they simply fall into it when the time is right, according to their own soul's plan of unfoldment. Sometimes one's natural mediumship abilities lie dormant until the right person activates their destined purpose to serve both worlds. I personally have very early memories of interacting with and observing Spirit as a child, but it was not until I had an NDE that the *awareness* of these gifts within me was reawakened.

After my transforming life event, my psychic and mediumship ability began to accelerate. The tendencies I'd always had as a child began to blossom and my connection to Spirit and my guides strengthened. More importantly, my love for Spirit deepened, and as a result, I became consciously aware of its continuous presence in my life. From that moment, I completely embraced my abilities and my passion for Spirit.

While my dedication to Spirit was sincere, I had a great deal to learn. I began working as a self-taught psychic without realizing I was also acting as a medium. I simply wasn't aware of the distinction between being psychic and being a medium. All of this would become clear to me, and I describe exactly how in later chapters.

In those early years of practice, I experienced many of the concerns that most new mediums have. Perhaps the biggest fear we all must face is the fear of self-delusion. We wonder at times: am I making this up? Am I receiving and transmitting the information accurately? Am I really communicating with Spirit people or guides who have crossed to the other side? These are common fears and cross the minds of all developing mediums at some point in their journey. Know that these fears are a normal phase of the work. Don't give up!

It's true that in the beginning of your development it's easy for your own mind to interfere with the messages you receive. Until we're fully trained, we cannot help but color the information we've received with material from our subconscious minds and our accumulated experiences. This often results in confusion, lack of trust and limited faith.

Mediumship development, however, is a *refinement* process; mastery of the mind is an absolute must. It is for this reason that I've chosen to write this book. My aim is to give you a basis of understanding not only of mediumship but also of yourself, and to normalize the experiences you're having so they no longer confuse you.

This book is intended to be *a starting point* for you to explore and deepen your mediumship development. It does not replace the relationship you will develop with your own Spirit guides and Spirit mentors; nor does it negate the need for you to find an actual teacher or mentor. My hope is that this book will be used as a guide and foundational text for your development, becoming a resource you can dip back into many times. It can be used to reinforce a topic you eventually study, or just to enhance your appreciation of the mechanics of mediumship. At the end of most chapters, you'll find exercises designed to help you heighten your psychic senses, develop and test relevant skills, establish useful routines, and more.

After reading this book, I encourage you to test and question everything you've learnt thus far, using your best discernment, to make sure that it rings true for you. While there are situations outlined in this book that all mediums will encounter at some point in their development, keep in mind that every medium's journey is unique.

It is my belief that we learn best through the sharing of our personal stories, for knowledge comes to life through experience. Bearing this in mind, I share in this book many anecdotes, each one chosen for the purpose of illustrating specific points and highlighting the teachings I've outlined. Of course, I have not used any real names or identifiers so that client confidentiality is preserved.

I would like to leave you with these words of encouragement before you commence your immersion. Your ability is unique to you and reflects the accumulation of all the experiences your soul has ever had. It's wonderful to admire other mediums and learn from them, but try to refrain from comparing yourself; it is not a race. Develop at your own pace and simply strive to be the best that you can be. If you place love and the desire to serve first and foremost, you simply cannot go wrong! Above all, trust yourself and trust your Spirit team of helpers; they will not let you down.

Now dive in and deepen your understanding and knowledge of all things Spirit. I would love to hear about your experiences and how this book may have assisted or inspired you. Please feel free to contact me with questions or comments via my Facebook page, www.facebook.com/IoannaSerpanos, or www.ioannaserpanos.com.

CHAPTER 1

# My story

*'Tell your story with your whole heart.'*
~ *Brené Brown*

At the time of my birth, my parents were renting a single room in a shared house, but by the time my younger brother was born, in 1971, we'd moved into a classic California bungalow. It was in this, our first home, that I first became aware of my abilities.

Born in the city of Hobart in Tasmania, Australia, my entrance into this world was a very humble one indeed. My parents emigrated from Greece to Australia in the late 1960s armed with just one suitcase; they left their families behind, seeking a better life for themselves and their baby son. They faced many trials and tribulations, like other migrants of the time, as they struggled to integrate and learn a new language and new customs, and make new friends.

My earliest memory of Spirit's presence is at the age of three or four, and they've been my companions ever since. I recall waking frequently at night to find that numerous 'people' would be moving around in my bedroom. Initially I would be petrified. My heart would pound and I'd hide under my blankets. After a while, curiosity would take over, and I'd peer out and watch them as they walked through my room, seemingly going about their business. They were dressed in different outfits from different eras, and I found myself simultaneously fascinated and frightened by them.

My young mind posed all kinds of questions: who were these people, and what were they doing in my room? Were they doing anything to me while I was asleep? What did they want of me? Eventually, fear would get the better of me, and back I'd hide under my bedding, trying to ignore their existence and willing myself to sleep. In the morning, I'd tell my father, but he'd just smile and say I must have dreamt it.

While walking in the hallway, often I'd hear my name called. I'd answer, assuming it was my mother, only to have her reply that she hadn't called me. Other times, I'd hear my name spoken by someone behind me, and would turn around to see who was there, knowing quite well that I was in my room alone. If I were home alone, I'd run through the hallway, or other parts of the house where these Spirit people were, as fast as possible. Ironically, later in life I reached a point where I felt comforted by their presence.

This continued until I was around seven and then I stopped seeing Spirit objectively; that is to say, I stopped seeing Spirit people standing in front of me with my physical eyes. From this point onwards, I began to only *feel* their presence; my vision shifted from my real eyes to my *mind's eye*. I didn't realize it at the time, but this was a natural phase in my development as a medium.

My interest in all things metaphysical ignited around the age of nine. An avid reader since the age of five, I used my pocket money to buy psychic magazines and books. I was fascinated by astrology, palmistry, ghost stories and anything that was psychic in nature. I stored these publications in the bottom of my wardrobe or hid them under my bed so that no one would know. Even at such a young age, I knew intuitively that I had to protect myself from people who might ridicule or misunderstand me.

I bought books on anything that was mysterious and began asking the big questions like 'Why are we here?' and 'Where did we come from?'. My thirst for knowledge was unquenchable; even today, I'm a wide and varied reader. I love to read and question what I've read – something I encourage all my students to do.

In a medium's family tree there will be at least one other family member who was known to have some ability; it is through the DNA that this ability is passed on. Sometimes it may miss a generation, so if you research for this, you may need to look further along your family tree. At other times, it may appear in another branch entirely. My maternal grandmother was the medium in my family tree and she now plays an active role in assisting me with my work from beyond the grave. My maternal grandfather was the empath or sensitive, and he too has passed on those traits to me.

## My soul training begins

My school years were tough. I was the only 'wog' kid in a predominantly British descendant populace. From year seven I was ostracized and bullied for having a Greek heritage. I survived on high alert, continuously assessing the environment in order to protect myself from the next attack.

I believe there are always blessings in the most arduous times. I now understand these experiences to be part of what I call 'soul training'. These challenges were opportunities that helped me develop certain skills I would need throughout my life. For example, I learnt how to think quickly on my feet, honing my mind and my reactions as I retaliated with witty yet pointed remarks. Perhaps more significantly, I learnt to be resilient and to trust my instincts, for I found I could rely on no one but myself. Spending many hours alone and on the outer fringes of social circles, I learnt to observe others and to study human nature and behavior. I learnt to empathize with and fight for the underdog, having had that experience myself.

Not all my school years were painful; I have many fond memories of my later years, particularly those spent in the engineering department at the University of Tasmania. The classes I took included quantum physics and energy waveforms. They were intellectually challenging but they inspired me and expanded my mind. The information I learnt then is now utilized by me in my teachings to explain how Spirit blends with us to pass on information and more. I believe that science and mathematics are the language of Spirituality and that they and Spirit are not mutually exclusive; I still love science and consider myself a science geek.

After graduating I focused on forging a career in automotive engineering, and my experiences with Spirit faded into the background. Upon reflection, I can see that even though the awareness of Spirit faded during those early years of my career, my psychic abilities did not. There were many instances in my career where I seemed to *know* things or be able to predict outcomes. Armed with this precognition, I would put plans or contingencies in place that came in very handy when dealing with my clients. I was always at least one step ahead of the game and often four or five steps ahead! I was considered 'lucky' and was told in performance reviews that my instincts were good. I always knew what the 'elephant in the room' was. Those hidden agendas relating to product outcomes were not so hidden for me.

This *knowing* about hidden things was something I had to learn to manage. During the conclusion of one particular meeting I turned to my colleague and said, 'So how are you and Jane (not her real name) going?' My colleague, with a most indignant look on his face, replied 'Jane? There's nothing going on with Jane and I!' I said, 'didn't you tell me you two were dating? I'm sure you did!' Looking rather worried he said, 'No, I most definitely did not!' As it turned out they were in fact secretly dating. At this point I realized that I had to be more aware of what was said to me verbally versus what I was picking up psychically.

My psychic skills enabled me to understand what the customer truly wanted and I received many awards and acknowledgments on behalf of the teams I managed. This resulted in my rapid progression up the corporate ladder. At the age of thirty-five I'd attained a General Manager role in a male-dominated industry – an incredible achievement since at that time there was only a 4 per cent representation of women in engineering.

Both during my school years and my professional career, I found myself in two main roles. The first is that I was either formally or informally mentoring or training others and the second was that I was thrust into leadership roles that involved speaking to large groups. I was always terrified of speaking to large groups of people. I now know that these activities were part of my soul training to realize my life purpose: to inspire and mentor others in the fields of mediumship and healing, and to speak before people in public settings. It is amazing how our life experiences prepare us for our calling, often without us realizing the reasons behind situations and events.

Having mentored countless people in the area of mediumship over the past five years, I've found that the soul training themes are consistent in many students' lives. Our soul often knows the whys and the wherefores well before our conscious mind has had the time to acknowledge what we're led to do.

## My seeking begins

On the surface, my life seemed amazing. I had a six-figure salary, a corporate leadership role and I travelled the world. I was living the dream, but deep inside I felt a yearning for something more. I felt empty, unfulfilled and very unhappy. My life had no meaning or purpose.

One day, during this period of yearning, I saw an advertisement in the local paper for an open day at a shiatsu college. I went along and found myself signing up for a diploma in shiatsu. At our first class a fellow student who was a psychic told me that I should find a development circle to join, since I too was a psychic. Hearing this for the first time raised my confidence and shifted my understanding of myself. It gave me a sense of direction, a place to plant myself from which I could move forward with momentum.

Armed with this new understanding about myself, I searched for a teacher who could guide my next steps. I joined a group that was predominantly focused on psychic development and started attending classes on a weekly basis. The group had been sitting together for a number of years, and I soon realized that I was a complete novice with much to learn. I recall during my first class sitting next to a woman who stood up, seemingly asleep, and started speaking in a deep, masculine voice as she passed on prophetic messages. I wondered what I'd gotten myself into! I now know that she was *trance communicating*, a topic I'll cover later in this book.

Although I wasn't sure what to make of this experience, fortunately I wasn't spooked, and I returned the following week. As time passed, I became immersed in learning how to explore and trust my psychic abilities – an important first step towards becoming a medium.

From a teaching perspective, my greatest learning in this circle was, ironically, what *not* to do. As a teacher it is vitally important to be aware of your own issues and to own those issues rather than projecting them onto your students. Clear boundaries, self-awareness and integrity are very important when you're entrusted with the development of another person. People are very vulnerable and impressionable when they're developing their ability; therefore, group leaders must be very aware of where they themselves are, Spiritually, mentally and emotionally.

Another blessing that came from that group was meeting my dear friend and fellow medium Sharon Lee. Sharon has worked tirelessly and with great passion for the Spirit world and, like me, has a deep love and reverence for Spirit. It was through Sharon that I was introduced to the renowned and well-respected medium and mentor Mavis Pittilla, who became my mentor. I'll describe more about that phase of my training later.

After sitting in this group for around two years I found that my proficiency and confidence had grown to the point where I was ready to begin seeing private clients at home. I recall giving a client a reading where I told her that her son would meet a girl; that two weeks later he would present her to his mother; and four weeks later he would marry her, on his birthday, in his mother's backyard! This had sounded ludicrous even to me but I had full confidence in my ability, honed from my class experiences, so I passed the information on. The client thanked me for her reading, but gave nothing away. Seven months later she returned for a reading and told me that when she'd first seen me she left thinking I was crazy and told all her friends not to bother with me, as I was a terrible psychic. She reminded me about my reading and told me that her son was forty years old and had never had a girlfriend. She felt that what I'd said was so unlikely that she refused to believe it. I replied, 'Well, you're back and now you wish to find out the sex of their baby!' She smiled brightly and confirmed the pregnancy. I then said, 'I hope you told your friends that I wasn't a terrible psychic.'

Still employed in the automotive industry I kept my new psychic life hidden; effectively I was in the 'psychic closet', like so many other people in this field, leading a double life. While I was honing and refining my abilities, I met my husband, who was supportive of my journey although he was never really able to truly understand it. Like many psychics and mediums, I was unable to be fully open about this part of my life without meeting resistance from family and social groups. This became isolating for me and contributed to my experiencing the sense of *psychic shame* that many intuitives feel.

I use this phrase to describe the feeling psychics have when they're unable to express what they're experiencing, even to those closest to them. Often, those with psychic gifts spend many years without anyone to really talk to about what they're seeing, hearing and knowing. They may question themselves and feel great anxiety at having to keep so much buried inside. It can be painful to face the fact that the majority of people do not understand what it's like to be a sensitive and how challenging it can be to walk through this world with this kind of ability. People who have such abilities often feel ostracized or regarded with suspicion until they find their niche in the world.

As time went by, I found that once I fully owned who I am, the reactions around me also changed. As with so many other things in life, we can never truly be our full and most authentic selves until we *choose* to do so!

The more I worked with clients, the more I came to understand that what I was doing was helping people navigate their lives. My clientele quickly grew through word of mouth while my dissatisfaction and restlessness within the corporate world intensified.

When I found out I was pregnant, I commenced manifesting my redundancy. I took out a bank statement and hand-wrote an additional line titled 'redundancy payout', with a figure that I expected to receive. I placed this revised statement on my vision board. Exactly one year and ten minutes after my maternity leave ended, I was made redundant, with a payout that matched the figure I had written on my bank statement.

## Coming out of the psychic closet

Following the birth of my daughter, I experienced another shift in my psychic development. The ability I'd had as a young girl returned, and once again I began to see Spirit objectively, manifesting before my physical eyes. This experience cemented my commitment to dedicating my life to the purpose of serving Spirit. Having been liberated from corporate confines, I was free to pursue my calling full-time; I knew that I would not be going back to a regular job. My passion for working with Spirit became all-consuming, and I was happier than I'd ever been.

I quickly secured commercial premises on a main street frontage and opened my healing center, which I called Experience Healing. There was to be no more hiding from my true identity as I stepped into what I was born to do. For the first time, I began to publicly call myself a psychic medium.

This brought me tremendous relief. The psychic shame I'd struggled with for so long finally diminished, and soon I found myself surrounded by like-minded people who were following a similar path. I began to see more clients and to host open days in the healing center, where I delivered informational seminars to the public. The feedback was positive, which spurred me on to expand my work. My confidence blossomed, and my thirst for more wisdom and knowledge deepened.

Three months into this new venture, my marriage disintegrated. My sorrow took me to a place of deepest and darkest despair. I wondered why I'd been guided to open this center only to be forced to close it just three months later. With tears in my eyes, I had to inform the practitioners who worked in the center that I was unable to keep the doors open and they would no longer have rooms to work from. To my great joy, these wonderful practitioners rallied around me, and made it possible for the center to continue providing services. I am forever grateful for their support and the courage they gave me at that difficult time in my life.

The stress of my marriage falling apart placed a tremendous emotional and physical strain on me. This, together with the deep grief I felt over losing my dream for a 'happy ever after', resulted in my having my near-death experience (NDE). Driving to work one morning after having dropped off my three-year-old daughter at her child-care center, I suddenly felt a gripping pain in my heart. My left arm fell away from the steering wheel, and I became hot, nauseous, panicked and in pain. Suddenly I felt myself transported through space and found I was floating above my body looking down at myself sitting in my vehicle. I was in four lanes of peak hour traffic, yet I was suspended in time.

As I floated there, I looked up to see an incredibly beautiful, loving, angelic face smiling down at me. Instantly, I was flooded with a feeling of tremendous peace. Accompanying this peace was the knowing that I was completely treasured and loved. The power of this love was like a huge magnet pulling me upwards towards unconditional, blissful, expansive Oneness. I had the surreal experience of being the single drop in the ocean as well as the whole ocean, simultaneously.

I asked this being (my Angel) to help me understand what was happening and, through some kind of mental communication, I was informed of what would occur if I chose to continue towards the light. It was as if a video was playing, showing me how my car would veer to the right and take out the three cars adjacent to me while the guy on my left would steer away from me, hitting the car on his left. My Angel then explained that if I continued towards the light, I would be taken home to rest, to be at peace and escape all pain. I knew I was being given the option. In that moment, the image of my precious three-year-old popped into my head and I found myself asking, 'But who will collect my daughter?'

The moment I had that thought, I found myself back in my body, highly distressed and in immense pain. My lips were moving in prayer, asking the Angel to help me. I realized everything I'd just experienced had occurred outside of time. My car had not veered, and I had continued to drive without causing injury to myself or to the other drivers. An incredible energy engulfed my head from behind and I heard a voice saying, 'You are having a heart attack, but you will be all right.' I was then instructed to drive straight to my workplace and told that my assistant would know what to do. I looked at the time in my car and it was 10 am. When I arrived at work, it was 10.05 am – a miracle, since it would normally have taken twenty minutes!

Just as I arrived, so did my assistant. She drove me immediately to the medical center, where it was confirmed that I'd had a heart attack. I developed pericarditis, a painful inflammation of the pericardium, the sheath covering the heart. My aorta, the main blood vessel of the heart, was swollen, but miraculously I did not have any damage to my heart muscle.

Some weeks later while receiving reiki for my condition, I found myself going into a deep meditative state. There, I relived my NDE, and was able to communicate with the beautiful, loving face of my Angel. I saw once again the space between both worlds and reviewed all that had happened. I realized in this review that I had been reminded of my life purpose: to teach and inspire others and to help them heal by being a vessel of unconditional love.

Ever-resilient and placing my full trust and faith into Spirit's hands I continued to run my healing center for another four wonderful years.

## My formal training begins

I was working full-time as a professional psychic, giving people readings about issues that were important to them such as their love life, career and of course predictive information about their futures. Most people consult a psychic to be reassured that the life choices they are making will work out for them.

During my work as psychic, I found myself doing the work of a medium without actually realizing what was occurring. For example, I was very much aware of my grandmother in Spirit and would often feel her around me, gently guiding me and giving me reassurance. As I conducted readings, I'd often see the departed loved ones of my clients. I'd share my impressions with them, but I didn't know that this part of the process was in fact called *mediumship*. To me, it was all part of being a psychic.

Gradually, I became aware that I had to formally develop my mediumship abilities. One morning, after running the center for four years, I awoke to hear Spirit say to me, 'You are not here to run a center.' I've learnt to trust my Spirit guides when they speak, so I closed my healing center and moved my practice back into an individually run business, freeing me up to focus on my mediumship training and service.

In January 2015 I was guided to attend a five-day residential mediumship course run by British medium Mavis Pittilla. At the time of booking this course, I had no idea that Mavis was one of the world's most respected mediums and mentors. I only knew in my heart I had to be there. Looking back, it is clear that Spirit guided me to this course so I could connect with a kindred soul in Mavis, who would ultimately help direct my passion for becoming a vessel for Spirit.

During this pivotal time with Mavis, I was able to gain a vocabulary and terminology that explained what I'd been experiencing as a self-taught medium. I came to understand the mechanics of mediumship practice and development, and I was able to put my experiences into context.

I came away with renewed enthusiasm for Spirit, but more importantly, a true confidence and belief in myself as a medium. I now understood the building blocks of mediumship development. In addition, I'd given my very first mediumship demonstration in front of an audience. If you'd asked me prior to the Sydney training to publicly demonstrate mediumship, the answer would have been a resounding 'No!' But under Mavis's tutelage, I was able to successfully take the stage and allow Spirit to do its work, and I have continued to do so.

In 2016, I travelled to the prestigious Arthur Findlay College in the UK to once again work with Mavis. My memories of my time there will remain in my heart forever; the atmosphere of the college was electrifying and to have sat in the room of renowned pioneer medium Gordon Higginson was such an honor. His Spirit presence was palpable as he regularly taught students from his library, which was my classroom for the duration of my stay. Since then, I have fully embraced the teaching and mentoring of mediums from all around the world. It's been an honor and a privilege to be able to witness the unfoldment of my students' abilities in their mediumship development.

I've learned that if we get out of our own way, Spirit will lead and inspire us to make choices in our lives that will ensure we are on our destined path. I believe that we are constantly in a refinement process of evolution. At the time of writing this book, I'm being called to mentor, heal and inspire others through my Spiritual work. While I do not know where this will ultimately lead me, I do intrinsically know that I'm following my soul's path and purpose for being. I also know that this path will change as time goes on, for life is always evolving. It's important that we remain open to the changes that come into our lives, not becoming too attached to any one set of conditions or outcomes.

CHAPTER 2

# Psychics and mediums

*'Close both eyes to see with the other.'*
*~ Rumi*

O ften the terms *psychic* and *medium* are used interchangeably, even though there is a very distinct difference between the two. There are other terms that are often confused or used incorrectly both by psychics and the general public alike, including clairvoyant, Spiritual medium, Tarot reader and Angel Card reader, to name just a few. In my opinion, all these labels fall under the two distinct categories of either psychic or medium.

## The difference between a psychic and a medium

To facilitate understanding of these categories I offer the following explanations.

A *psychic* makes contact with an *incarnate Spirit*. That is to say, they connect with the Spirit that is housed inside a living human body. Psychics essentially blend or attune with the sitter's auric field and read that person's history, current surrounding conditions and most probable future, based on the energy that is seen in that snapshot in time. I use the words 'most probable' as I am allowing for the *law of free will* that is a birthright of us all. *We all have the ability, the responsibility and the power to make decisions that will shape our future potential.*

*A medium* connects and interacts with a *discarnate person*; one who has passed into the world of Spirit. A medium will blend not with the aura of a living person but the aura of a person from the Spirit world and will deliver any messages the Spirit person may wish to pass on. In addition, the medium will usually describe physical characteristics and personality traits, and relay personal stories about the Spirit person by way of proof of survival.

It is my belief that we are all psychic; it is in our DNA and we are all born with this ability. Like any skill set, some of us are very practiced and proficient in it and some of us are not. We can compare this with something like singing, for example. If we can speak, then we can also sing, but some of us are destined to do most of our singing in the shower while others go on to become world famous performers. Our innate psychic abilities are similar to this. We all have them, but we're able to access them to different degrees.

Most people use their psychic senses on a daily basis, often without awareness that they're doing so. The clue is in the language we use. Have you ever heard yourself say, 'I had a gut feeling about this', or perhaps, 'I knew that was going to happen!' We use these common sayings without realizing that we are, in fact, engaging our psychic senses.

I also believe we all have the capacity to be mediums, but not all of us have the *desire* or, more importantly, the *calling* to do so. Mediumship is an act of service, and the call to be a medium is similar to the call a priest or other member of the clergy may have. The work involves far more than delivering messages that are passed on from our loved ones beyond the veil; it also brings great emotional, mental, Spiritual and even physical healing.

Psychics and mediums work with different kinds of energy. A psychic deals with the energy of a human body, tuning into the person's thoughts and feelings. This energy is naturally denser than the energy of those who have passed on and are no longer using a human body. After interacting with this denser energy, psychics may find themselves feeling tired or depleted. This is not to say they aren't uplifted and thrilled that they were able to help someone in need, but this upliftment is separate from the natural fatigue that occurs as a result of psychically aligning oneself with the emotional, physical and mental energies of a human being. This fatigue may occur more often in the early stages of a psychic's work. As one becomes more adept at managing energy, the fatigue may lessen, much like muscle fatigue diminishes when you're consistently exercising in the gym. Ensuring regular breaks and doing activities that refresh personal energy is key for a psychic to remain in balance.

The medium works with Spirit energy rather than physical energy. Since a Spirit person is free of the body, their auric field is lighter and vibrates at a higher frequency. When a medium interacts with such an auric field, she/he tends to feel energized rather than fatigued, because the vibration of the Spirit world is naturally invigorating and self-replenishing. When a medium is sitting in the power of Spirit, illness and fatigue disappear for the duration of the contact. If you watch a medium work, you'll notice that they appear more energetic, youthful and vibrant, as if they're glowing. Of course, once they come out of the power, any pre-existing ailment unfortunately resurfaces!

While the energy experienced during a mediumship reading may be refreshing, this does not mean that mediums do not need to carefully manage their time and general state of wellbeing. Mediums are responsible for maintaining their own emotional equilibrium and overall health so they can be the best conduit possible during a reading. When you undertake the study of mediumship, it soon becomes apparent that without regular self-care and the pure intention to serve, the demands of being a vessel for Spirit will soon overwhelm the individual. A great deal of time and dedication go into preparing yourself to be available to Spirit at this level, and this only increases once you're actively working in the field. In other words, becoming a medium is not a one-time event, but requires constant vigilance if you are to maintain integrity, stamina, patience and, most of all, compassion. The medium is also responsible for her/his continuing expansion of consciousness, so that they do not become stagnant. Just as a physician takes the Hippocratic oath to 'do no harm' and commits to staying abreast of the newest medical information, so is the dedicated medium expected to commit to her own growth and continuing Spiritual education. These are all things to consider when the study of mediumship is undertaken.

It's part of the ethical creed of Spiritual workers to be clear with clients about the nature of their work. If you're using your psychic abilities in a reading, say so. Likewise, if you're connecting to Spirit and bringing forth messages for a person, explain this as well. Part of studying mediumship is learning discernment between the two abilities. If you aren't sure, a good rule of thumb is to notice where your information seems to be coming from. If you're being drawn to a living person and sensing their thoughts, their aura or their feelings, you're doing psychic work. If, however, your initial connection takes place with Spirit and then you give the information from Spirit to a person, you're working as a medium.

In some cases, a reader may conduct a session that combines the two. Again, it's best to explain to the sitter where the information is coming from as you give it: either from Spirit directly or from the physical person's auric field.

Although the work of a medium may be your ultimate goal, always remember that a solid development of the psychic abilities will give you a strong foundation upon which to build your mediumship. The mediumship component will blossom out of these roots.

## The psychic senses

It is through the psychic senses that communication with Spirit is initiated and strengthened; therefore, any foundational development work should focus on honing and refining your psychic skills. The psychic senses are:

- **Clairvoyance** – clear seeing: the medium receives images or pictures from Spirit, which they then pass on to the sitter. These pictures most often appear in the medium's mind (through the third eye), but in some instances, mediums are able to see Spirit objectively with their physical eyes, as if Spirit were standing right in front of them.

- **Clairaudience** – clear hearing: the medium uses their mind to hear words, sounds and phrases spoken by the person in Spirit, which they pass on to the sitter. This is very much like listening to the Spirit person's thoughts as they're transferred inside your own head. Very often, the medium will hear the Spirit person's voice, accent or tone. Often mediums will have one particular ear that's more attuned to hearing Spirit. For me, I hear Spirit through my right ear. Once again, there are some mediums that are able to hear Spirit objectively with their physical ears.

- **Claircognizance** – clear knowing: this is one of the harder clairs to define in that the medium simply knows information about a sitter who've they've had no prior exposure to. It's as if the knowledge suddenly drops into the medium's consciousness, seemingly out of nowhere. This claircognizance can be about topics totally unrelated to the medium's own experiences, field of expertise or knowledge.

- **Clairsentience** – clear feeling: the medium, through the blending of their aura with the Spirit person's aura, is able to feel emotions and ailments the Spirit person experienced while alive as if they had been superimposed onto and into the body of the medium. By feeling these emotions and physical symptoms, the medium is able to accurately convey how the person in Spirit physically felt in life.

- **Clairalience** – clear smelling: the medium is able to detect scents from the world of Spirit such as cigarette smoke, perfume, hobby-related odors or cooking smells, to name but a few. These smells are usually considered signature scents associated with the person when they were in a physical body.
- **Clairgustance** – clear tasting: with this technique, the medium is able to discern the taste of certain food or drinks that the Spirit person was known for, as if the medium was physically eating that food.

## Development circles

A psychic development circle is a place where you can practice your psychic skills. There are many styles of circles from which to choose, be it online or a traditional home circle. If you're just embarking on your development journey, then joining a circle is a good way to become familiar with your abilities.

A good development circle will be led by a facilitator who's skilled enough to be able to recognize and assess your current skill set and then determine which exercises or set of practices will assist your growth. This leader should foster confidence, trust and belief in you and also in your Spirit team. They should be comfortable with you asking questions, testing knowledge and practices, and being discerning.

It is imperative that the circle leader ensures that each circle participant is given equal opportunity to develop. A leader should also be proficient in what they are teaching and be able to demonstrate this. They themselves should be open to continuous learning and research and not be so mired in dogma that they're unable to progress. I've always encouraged my students to find out for themselves if my style and way of teaching suits them or not. If it doesn't, that's perfectly okay. There is not a *one size fits all* style in mediumship; we each bring our own flavor to it. Part of the Spiritual journey is to understand ourselves and find the niche where we belong, which includes finding teachers and fellow seekers with whom we have a natural affinity.

If you're able to find a development circle that truly resonates with you, it can be a life-changing experience. You'll know that you've joined the circle that's right for you when there's a strong feeling of coming *home*. You'll feel seen and heard, nurtured and respected, and your soul will instinctively sense that you're meant to be there. Practicing mediumship among like-minded people yields benefits far beyond the technical skills mastered. It boosts your confidence so you're able to stretch beyond your current range of ability, and allows you to openly exercise your psychic muscles.

An effective development circle is a place where the freedom to experiment and try new things will allow you to hone your craft and master new skills while being supported by the group leader and other circle members. The accumulated group energies of a solid development circle will propel your growth far more rapidly than if you were to attempt it in isolation.

There's nothing more satisfying for me than to see a developing fledgling medium grow their wings and soar with confidence. To see the look of amazement when they move from being insecure about their abilities to a state of absolute trust in themselves and their Spirit team is a wonderful thing. The blossoming of an inspired unfoldment is truly a blessing to facilitate and witness.

So what can you expect from a typical development circle? Each group leader will add their own personal style to the process, but there are some standard practices in most circles. These include an opening meditation or prayer, a series of practical exercises designed to strengthen your psychic skills, and a period of time to actually link to

Spirit and practice giving readings. Most circles run for about two hours, and at the end of that time, a closing prayer or final meditation is conducted. While it's important that the circle has a solid structure, what's far more important is the level of support, acceptance, encouragement and positivity within the group. In addition, the circle should stimulate your mind and heart so that you feel you're continuously learning and progressing. While it's normal to have peaks, valleys and plateaus along the Spiritual path, prolonged stagnancy is a sign that it's time to reassess where you are and what you're doing. It may be that you simply need to motivate yourself beyond your resistance point. Then again, it might be time to find a new practice circle or to add another kind of class to your experience. At times, you may find that you actually need to take a brief sabbatical from your Spiritual studies to recalibrate your body and mind. Stagnancy can come from becoming too comfortable in your routines. It's easy to settle into what we're familiar with, resisting anything that challenges our status quo. As with the rest of life, we must remain open to change and fresh information if we are to grow.

The development circle you choose should feel aligned with your values and principles. Trust is the most important key ingredient, followed by ethics and integrity. A properly run circle will foster in you the confidence to identify, get to know and understand your own Spirit team, who are instrumental in guiding and training you. Egos, if they are present, must be managed by the facilitator so that everyone has equal access to learning. It is at times necessary to face the fact that there are many well-meaning circle leaders who may genuinely believe it is their calling to run a circle, but in truth are not suited for the work. It's up to us to have the discernment to recognize if the circle is a healthy, supportive one or exists only to satisfy someone's ego, financial needs or quest for power over others. If at any time it becomes unsafe or intimidating for you to be in a circle, then leave immediately. If you're being undermined in any way, made to feel insecure or inadequate, then be courageous enough to leave and seek another circle. An engineering mentor once said to me, 'In engineering drawing, if it doesn't look right, it's not right.' What he was saying was that I had to use not just my technical knowledge but also my judgment and gut instincts.

I've seen many students give their power away to other circle leaders. Sadly, I've also seen students be damaged by leaders. In one instance, one of my students had been told in another circle that she was keeping Spirit earthbound due to her negative energy! This circle was highly critical of her and her efforts, causing her to doubt herself and to move into fear, thus damaging the quality of her mediumship. Although it can be useful to be part of a learning group, do not lose yourself within the group. Back yourself and trust your instincts; be responsible for your own wellbeing and development. It doesn't matter how famous or renowned a teacher may be, or how many people have recommend them. If it doesn't feel right for you, then go with your own intuition.

If you do choose to sit in a circle, then make sure that you're committed to the process. Turn up to each session and follow through with the exercises and practices between sessions. I've always said to my students you get out what you put in. Remember that you're there to give as well as receive, and dedicate yourself to bringing the highest intentions to every meeting. Be a team player. Support and assist your fellow students, acting with kindness and humility. Remember that you're there to collectively progress for the good of all, not to compete with one another. When circle participants compare themselves to others, it can result in feelings of inferiority or superiority. I wholeheartedly encourage you to refrain from doing this, as it will delay your development. Keep in mind that we're all unique and bring with us a particular set of talents, strengths and skills, the perfect blend for us to become the best mediums we can be. Offer all that you have and all that you are to Spirit – that's all they ask of us. Then trust that as long as we're willing and committed, Spirit will do the rest.

This willingness cannot be overstressed. Studying mediumship is like studying any subject: if you turn up to class for two hours per week and then don't put into practice what you've learnt, you won't progress in your development, nor in your career. The Spirit world will make every effort to assist in your development if they can see that you're committed to the process, helpful to others, and motivated not by ego but the true desire to serve.

Once you have a good practical understanding of your psychic skills, then it's time to seek out more specialized mediumship training. With a good grounding in psychic skills, you'll be able to progress far more rapidly in your mediumship development. Seek out mentors who have a proven track record in the field and who embody your own values. Again, ask Spirit to guide you to the right mentor and to help you maintain discernment about who is the best connection for you at this stage in your development.

I've offered these cautions not to put fear in your heart, but because any important step we take in life requires discernment. Perform your due diligence, and then walk onward in faith, hope and joy, trusting in Spirit and grateful for the wonderful path to which you have been led.

**Exercises**

1. Identify the color that you are most drawn to or wear the most. Reflect on how that color makes you feel, and why. Now repeat for the color you like the least. What do these colors mean to you personally, and what do you think they represent in the universal sense? Develop your own color library of meaning.

2. Place a number of different-colored lengths of ribbon on a ring or safety pin. Have your partner close their eyes and choose three ribbons; each one represents past, now and future of the person who is choosing. Read each of the chosen ribbons and pass on any thoughts, impressions or feelings to your partner to receive their feedback on accuracy.

3. Practice attuning your ear to open your clairaudience by sitting quietly with your eyes closed for 1 minute. Listen to every sound you hear and then open your eyes and list all the sounds you heard. Now set the intention to open your clairaudience and repeat the exercise, noting how many additional sounds you hear. Sounds may include your breathing, traffic noise, dogs barking, etc.

4. Listen to a piece of instrumental music. Focus on one particularly instrument and tune out the rest. This exercise further refines your clairaudience.

5. To practice your clairvoyance skills head outside on a cloudy day. Lie on the grass and get centered, with the intention that you wish to open your clairvoyance. Study the clouds and see if a picture forms in the cloud formations. Take note of what appears.

6. Have a friend place ten random items on a table when you're not present, or study a picture of ten random items. Close your eyes and then visualize those items and the order they appear

in. Recount them to your friend or say them aloud while recording your voice so that you can verify your answer.

7. To develop your clairsentience, ask a friend to show you a picture of someone you don't know. Gaze into the eyes of that person and tune into the feelings you're experiencing. Do you feel happy? Sad? Frustrated? Angry? Pass on your feelings and ask your friend to verify your answers.

8. The next time you find yourself waiting in a queue, try this: without turning around, feel how close the person is behind you, how tall they are and how wide. Do they feel feminine or masculine? Turn around and check your answer.

9. Practice your claircognizance by watching quiz shows. Set the intention that you're working on your knowing, and answer questions (before the show participant does) on topics that you've never studied and know nothing about.

10. Finally, to practice your clairgustance and clairalience try food dishes from many and varied cultural kitchens. Focus on each flavor and try to isolate various taste profiles, such as sweet, sour, bitter and salty. Further refine your ability by trying to identify key ingredients and subtle flavors.

CHAPTER 3

# The aura

*'Be consistent in maintaining an aura of grace and love.'*
*~ Meggan Roxanne*

The aura is an energy field composed of multiple layers of color and vibration that surrounds the body. The center of the aura is actually the physical body itself; therefore, the body is the first and densest or heaviest band of vibration. As we move out from the physical body we're enveloped and overlapped by successive fields of energy that become lighter and finer in vibration. These layers include our mental or thought body, our emotional body, and our Spiritual body.

Within the aura there are energy vortices (spinning wheels of energy) known as chakras. Each of the seven main chakras is located along our energetic spinal cord and emits a particular color aligned to the rainbow and consequently has a particular frequency.

A person's aura contains the residue of every experience they've ever had, through every faculty available to them. In other words, the aura contains every thought, every feeling, every sensation and every karmic condition the person was born with and has accumulated in their lifetimes.

We are often subconsciously attracted (or repelled) by the color we need the most. Certain colors have healing powers that are best suited to specific parts of our psyche or body. We're attracted to these colors when we feel ready to accept the healing they offer, and are repelled when we're resistant to the healing of that aspect of ourselves. Taking note of how we choose and reject colors in our surroundings and even in our wardrobe can teach us a great deal about ourselves.

I've experienced this personally with the color yellow. This was a color I had an aversion to for many years, until I had a deep healing occur in my solar plexus area. Since that time, I've grown to appreciate the color yellow and have incorporated it into my clothing and environment. While healing has its own timetable and cannot be forced, analyzing how certain colors fit into our lives can help us open up to the areas of ourselves that need healing the most.

Most psychics can see or perceive auric colors, and by developing an understanding of what those colors symbolize, they can effectively read the general condition of the person, their history and what is happening in their current lives. Many look to Nature for clues regarding color meaning. It's true that certain colors in the aura and each chakra have universal meanings that all teachers and students agree upon; however, just as a piece of silver can become tarnished and then brilliant again after polishing, so can auras. You may learn that gold represents a high form of Spiritual service, but if you see a tarnished gold, your intuition may tell you that this person is moving towards Spiritual service but haven't fully arrived as they're struggling with some residual heavy vibrations in their lives. A light, vibrant green is typically indicative of recent new growth and eagerness for learning, but if the green is pale or sickly, your subjective interpretation of the color should be applied to better help the individual. Always go with what a color feels like to you and what your Spirit team is guiding you to understand. I would encourage you to develop a personal relationship with shades of color and understand the effect of those colors on you.

Some readers can see auras with their physical eyes, while others perceive them in their mind's eye, tuning in to the emotions emanated by the colors. I've personally developed the ability to see aura with my physical eyes, but this has taken time and training. Do not be discouraged if you can't initially see the aura; you may be able to perceive it through other psychic faculties, and as time passes you will become more skillful at this.

Reading the aura is a useful tool to master so that you can best serve your client, your student and yourself. If you have aspirations for teaching mediumship, you'll be able to discern what psychic faculties are present in your students by observing the aura and then intelligently guide your student and help them develop by pinpointing areas for improvement.

I believe a solid mastery of color in the auric field will allow maximum growth potential for developing psychics and mediums alike. Any efforts made early in your development will cement your future career as a working medium and psychic.

**Exercises**

1.  Place yourself in front of a mirror and take a moment to center yourself. Begin by gazing at your reflection, with the intention that you wish to see your aura. Gaze at the area above or to the side of your head and look for a halo of energy around your head. Hint: try to relax your eyes while looking, without concentrating too intensely. With time and practice you'll begin to perceive a white halo. With further practice, you'll be able to perceive more colors.

2.  Have someone sit in natural light against a white background (wall, screen, sheet). Gaze at them with a soft focus, directing your attention on the area surrounding the person's head. With practice, the aura about an inch (2.5 centimeters) around the head may become visible. Ask the person to think of something that makes them joyful, then something that makes them anxious, and see if you can see a change in the color. You can also have them attempt to widen or contract their aura without telling you which they are doing, to perceive if your awareness of this is correct.

3.  Practice blending intuitively with the aura of a partner by visualizing your aura overlapping theirs. Choose to identify one or two things from each color band – mental (their thoughts), emotional (feelings), physical (body) and Spiritual (soul). Share your impressions about their aura to ascertain how accurate your reading is.

CHAPTER 4

# Styles of mediumship

*'Life is eternal, love is immortal, and death is only a horizon ...
and a horizon is nothing save the limit of our sight.'*

*~ Rossiter Worthington Raymond*

Over time, each medium develops their own unique style of mediumship. Your way of communicating with Spirit and expressing the messages you receive is, and always will be, unique to you and you alone. This is because you have your own kind of *relationship* with Spirit that no one else can duplicate. This relationship has emerged out of the garden of your personal life experiences and personality traits. The many influences that have come and gone in your life have led you to fashion a perspective about Spiritual matters that is unique to you.

Whatever your style may be, always remember that it's absolutely perfect for you! There can never be two mediums that are identical, although in more recent times I've had the misfortune of witnessing developing mediums cloning the style of more established or renowned mediums and thereby losing their own unique style. I hope you will treasure your special way of relating to Spirit enough to not let this happen to you. There's no reason to feel inferior if your style is not like another's, even someone whom you admire greatly. Remember, there is no one medium for everyone, but everyone will find that one medium who is best for them.

Let me share my personal style of mediumship with you, not because it's better but because it's an example of how unique each style truly is.

I call my style *soul-to-soul* mediumship, and this is how it works: firstly, I consider my primary client to be Spirit, and I approach my reading with the motivation that I am there to be in service to the will of Spirit, acting as a vessel or mouthpiece for whatever Spirit wishes to communicate to the sitter. If I were to open myself first to the sitter, I would receive impressions from them through my psychic abilities rather than from the highest source, Spirit. When my soul is open first to Spirit, I also know that my own thoughts and opinions can be bypassed so that the information I receive will have as little influence from me personally as possible. Through working in this way, I'm not reflecting the mind or desires of the sitter; nor am I reflecting my own thoughts and preferences. The goal of this method is to produce information that is evidential (can be verified and proven) and as is clear (untainted by my thoughts) as possible. This can also result in the sitter being told things that are not exactly what they thought they'd hear from me, for I try not to censor what Spirit chooses to communicate.

From this starting point, I then connect with the sitter's energy, building that bridge between Spirit and them, with me as the conduit between. Once the sitter feels the energy of Spirit passing through me to them, their soul awakens in trust, for it recognizes Spirit for what it truly is – authentic and loving. This openness is necessary if the sitter is to truly hear and *understand* at a deep level what Spirit is trying to tell them. Trust and openness also enables the sitter to receive Spirit's healing power and to really sense the presence of their loved one as well as recognize their loved one's unique traits.

Soul-to-soul mediumship may appear a little less dazzling than some other popular methods, but I've found that if I stay true to my own style, carefully connecting in this way, the results are accuracy, relevance and healing.

Each medium will uncover their own style as they develop, growing in understanding about themselves and what Spirit wants of them. Each of us has a special niche to fill in the field of Spiritual work. It's a true joy when we discover that niche and fully embrace it, rather than becoming distracted by trying to imitate the style of others.

Throughout time, there have been many pioneers in the field of mediumship. A little research will uncover many great names and their respective achievements within the sphere of Spiritualism. In modern times, many excellent mediums have become recognized television or celebrity mediums. People have conflicting opinions about these mediums; personally, I have great respect for them, for they had to break into an area of the media that was not previously open to mediums. Many of these mediums had to really wow an audience to gain credibility, interest and attention. It took a great deal of courage for them to go before the public eye, enduring skepticism and at times condemnation, in order to pave the way for those who would come after them. Because of their willingness to share their mediumship on a global scale, they were able to bring the concept of life after life to the masses as never before. There is certainly a place for this type of mediumship. Celebrity mediums made it more acceptable for mediums in general to communicate through the internet, live feeds, YouTube videos and more. As technology changes, so too will Spirit's methods of delivering information.

No matter what your style is, rest assured that the world of Spirit is very pleased that you're willing to give your time and energy to stand up on their behalf. They will always support you in your endeavors if you strive to serve with pure motives and a truly humble heart.

This is why I encourage my students to put aside their fears and conduct an experiment with Spirit. What do I mean by an experiment?

Quite simply, just have a go and see what happens! Use your practice circle to take a risk and try something new. This is the place where you want to feel completely free to open your heart and mind to Spirit and allow what comes forth to be expressed. This is where you want to refine your technique before you present publicly; the demonstration platform is not always the best place to be experimental! Within the development circle, I recommend exploring all three pillars of mediumship: the *messages*, the *healing* and the *philosophy*. (These will be covered in more depth in subsequent chapters.) To be the best medium we can be, we want to balance these three pillars within ourselves and ultimately infuse them into our readings so that those we read for receive all aspects of Spirit's truth.

Below, I describe the broad categories of mediumship as I currently understand them to be, so that you can perhaps identify how you're currently working or how you may wish to work in the future. Please note that the word *sitter* refers to the person who is having the reading, and of course the *medium* is the person giving the reading.

## Mental or Spiritual mediumship

This style of mediumship is when the medium uses their mental faculties to blend with and to communicate with the person in the Spirit world. They pass on messages utilizing at least one of the following clairs (spiritual senses), but usually more than one, in combination:

- **clairvoyance** – clear seeing
- **clairaudience** – clear hearing
- **claircognizance** – clear knowing
- **clairsentience** – clear feeling
- **clairalience** – clear smelling
- **clairgustance** – clear tasting.

(See Chapter 2, 'Psychics and mediums', for more in-depth explanations of each of these psychic senses.)

Let me share an example of how psychic senses can combine during a reading. I was conducting a demonstration at a local Spiritualist church when a woman in Spirit connected with me. The first thing she shared with me was the *taste* of homemade lemonade (clairgustance). She then allowed me to look through her eyes as she stood at her kitchen sink and I could *see* (clairvoyance) the lemon tree in her backyard. I could also see her two granddaughters playing near the tree. I then *heard* (clairaudience) her two granddaughters laughing, as they loved to play around that tree. My heart opened in response to this happy sight, and I could *feel* (clairsentience) the love she had for her granddaughters. I knew that she had shown her love by making the lemonade they loved to drink.

In this example you can see that four of the six clairs were used to receive the information that this Spirit woman wanted to share. The lemonade was the defining thing that allowed the recipient of that reading (her son-in-law) to know with certainty that I had his mother-in-law with me, since she was renowned for her homemade lemonade.

Spirit is always ready to communicate information through every one of the available clairs; it depends on the medium's style as to how many of these senses are used. Most mediums have at least one, if not two, naturally developed psychic faculties that become the core tools in their psychic toolkit. With regular practice under the guidance of a mentor, they're able to build upon what they've already developed naturally and explore other psychic faculties, thus expanding their skill set.

I've come across many developing mediums that *feel* quite profoundly, yet are highly discouraged because they cannot *see*. They believe that they're not as developed as other mediums because they're unable to utilize their clairvoyance. It's my personal opinion that the most effective mediums are these clairsentient (feeling) mediums, for their deep compassion helps their sitter to open up at the heart level. As humans, one of the highest gifts we can give to another is the gift of empathy, of truly understanding what the other is going through. A clairsentient medium touches the sitter's heart, which is essential for healing to occur.

Mental or Spiritual mediums usually employ their skills by conducting private sittings in an office setting, a private home or, in more recent times, over the telephone or through online applications such as Skype or Facebook. Mental mediums often demonstrate their skills publicly in a Spiritualist church setting, at expos or psychic fairs, or at their very own public event or show. Their goal is to bring forth information that is so specific and detailed it would be impossible for them to guess or know beforehand.

The next type of mediumship I wish to explore is the field of physical mediumship, where Spirit communicates with their intended recipients through physical manipulation of the environment around them. This type of mediumship was highly popular in the early pioneering days of mediumship but unfortunately (in my opinion) it has not made great leaps forward in more modern times.

## Physical mediumship

Physical mediumship is a method in which observable events and characteristics are manifested in a reading. It's regarded today as one of the most controversial forms of mediumship. In times past, it was also considered rare and marginal, yet was more openly embraced. Skepticism has built up around this method due to the unusual nature of events that occur during a reading, as well as the fraudulent actions of some unscrupulous people falsely claiming to have this ability. While discernment is important in regard to this field, bear in mind that authentic physical mediums do exist.

During a physical mediumship reading, those in attendance may see with their natural eyes the transfiguration of Spirit via ectoplasm as well as *apports* (objects that appear and/or disappear). They may also witness movement of items in the room such as trumpets, tables, balls, or other things chosen for the demonstration. In addition, they may hear audible, discarnate, out-of-body voices during the reading.

Historically, physical mediums have taken years to develop their skills in closed, home-based development circles. A closed circle is not open to the public and is made up of a group of people who meet on a regular basis. Such circles require extremely dedicated and trusted sitters, since they may sit seemingly in vain with absolutely nothing happening for many months. Consistent and regular sitting is imperative if the ability to channel physical phenomena is to occur, for the sitters' energies must be harmonized with the Spirit team who are endeavoring to work with the medium for this unique purpose. In addition, the medium must develop to the point where their energy is high enough in frequency and quality for manifestation of Spirit to occur. Since it takes a lot of psychic energy and an extremely long time to develop physical mediumship, it is reported that it can take years off a medium's life. This may be one of the reasons physical mediumship is not as prevalent as mental mediumship.

The sitters who surround a physical medium are vital to the process. They support the medium by providing their own energy to bolster the connection to Spirit. The medium usually connects with their Spirit team prior to demonstrating and receives advice as to where to place each of the sitters in the circle to balance the circle's total energies. In this way, the sitters effectively become *battery packs* for the Spirit world. Over time, a level of trust and attunement is developed between the medium, supporting sitters and the Spirit team, which eventually enables physical manifestations.

This type of mediumship was far more common during the Victorian era than today. Many rules and protocols and a particular etiquette have developed around the process of physical mediumship. Early pioneers, together with their Spirit teams, established these protocols, and modern mediums continue to adhere to them. These special processes include practicing in total darkness (or under a red light for certain applications) and having certain controls placed on the medium. The need for a *control* arose to counter the negativity associated with those who have been caught playing tricks on people, pretending to create physical phenomena. These controls may include tying the medium's hands and legs to their chair or placing them in a dark cabinet that has been independently inspected. In a circle that is open to the public, designated sitters will hold the medium's hands and legs to reassure the group that the medium has not moved from their seat at any time during the session.

## Séances – effects that may be observed

A séance is a gathering of sitters who are seeking to witness physical mediumship. Listed below are a number of experiences one may or may not have during a séance. What occurs during the séance is a result of Spirit's assessment of what is needed by the sitters and the medium's background and training.

### Temperature differential

In some instances, if Spirit is present, psychic breezes may be felt moving around the room. This coolness is usually felt around and below the knees. It is my understanding that Spirit will use our body heat as an energy source, hence the sensation of coolness. To someone unfamiliar with this process, it may seem strange and frightening, associated with ghosts and other fear-based concepts. You may rest assured that the coolness has a scientific explanation and is not harmful or abnormal.

### Psychic smells or aromas

Certain scents once associated with a Spirit person, such as a particular perfume or tobacco, may be detected in the séance. While this may be startling at first, it is truly a wonderful, tangible confirmation of our loved one in Spirit being present, something to be treasured and valued greatly.

## Ectoplasm and transfiguration

Many mediums find it necessary to prepare their bodies before manifesting ectoplasm. They may use methods such as fasting, resting, meditating, or entering a trance state in the days before or just prior to holding a séance. Ectoplasm is a milky white, vaporous substance that emerges from the orifices of the medium's body, usually from the solar plexus, mouth, eyes, ears or nose. It has a distinctive smell to it, and occasionally takes on different colors. The ectoplasm may manifest as a visible general cloudiness near the medium, or, if the energy is high enough, Spirit may use it to create an ectoplasmic mask where many faces or features may pass over the medium's face in rapid succession so sitters may see and recognize many of their departed loved ones. This is known as transfiguration. Transfiguration also applies to the hands of the medium. In this case, people will be able to watch the medium's hands change in size according to the hand size of the Spirit person. This phenomenon is wonderful to witness, as Spirit will usually change only one hand of the Medium while the other remains the same for the purpose of contrast.

## Materializations

Spirit may also use ectoplasm to materialize as a full form, possessing all the defining characteristics of a loved one, including facial features, clothing and other details. This form will stand in front of the sitter they wish to communicate with and will usually be recognizable as a loved one from the Other Side. To achieve materialization, the physical medium will usually, as mentioned, sit within an enclosed area called a cabinet. It is thought that the cabinet helps to contain and focus the energies required for materialization. There is usually a curtain in front of the cabinet, which can be parted in order for the sitters to see what's going on inside. When a materialization is about to happen, however, the curtains are closed.

If a Spirit person fully materializes, they will walk away from the medium, leave the cabinet, and connect with the sitters. A cord of ectoplasm linking the Spirit form with the physical medium will remain, which can often be seen by everyone. This ectoplasmic cord can be likened to the umbilical cord of a fetus.

Materialized Spirit has been shown to have the ability to walk out among the sitters, talk to them via direct voice, and to touch, hug, dance with and even kiss them. In some instances it has been reported that materialized Spirit has created fingerprints of their own materialized hands, moved heavy objects, and some have been witnessed passing through walls.

It is reported that if a bright light source is suddenly introduced when a medium is producing ectoplasm, the medium may sustain burns or physical injury. This is why a séance room is completely blacked out and why once the séance commences, no one is allowed to leave the room under any circumstance

Some physical mediums report feeling nauseous, tired or 'hungover' after a séance where ectoplasm has been produced. These effects can last from only a few hours to, in some cases, several days. Needless to say, this type of mediumship is not for the faint-hearted.

*Table-tipping*

This phenomenon is rather well known among Spiritualists. The medium and sitters are positioned around a table with their fingertips placed lightly on top of the table, each person's little finger touching the next sitter's thumb. Again, the medium will choose the order of the sitters in the circle to ensure that the best flow of energy is generated. The quality of this flow will determine how much energy is made available to the Spirit world to use in their manifestation of phenomena.

The protocol for communication with Spirit via the table is defined by the medium. For example, a 'yes' may be indicated when the table tips towards the right-hand side of the medium while a tip to the left may indicate a 'no'. Or the medium may define a 'yes' as two knocking sounds upon the table and 'no' as one knock. Of course, the medium will explain the protocol for communication before the séance begins.

It is not uncommon for a table to walk across a room on its legs or levitate into the air. To achieve levitation, it will turn in a circular motion as the energy is built up under the table, and then lift off the ground, clearly demonstrating the power of Spirit. In some cases, people have received a *table hug* from their loved ones, where the table tips completely over into the lap of the recipient! Seeing an inanimate object move in such a way to express love from the Spirit world can be very emotional for the recipient. It's remarkable how the table's behavior can reflect the Spirit person, moving gently or assertively in accordance with their character and individual traits.

*Trumpet*

The modern day trumpet is basically an aluminum cone with a hole in each end that acts as a simulated *voice box* for Spirit to use. It is painted with fluorescent paint or has fluorescent tape applied to its ends so it may be seen at all times by those in the circle, who are sitting in the dark. The trumpet is placed in the middle of the circle; when Spirit wishes to speak through it, the trumpet levitates and moves directly in front of the person who is to receive the communication. Spirit's voice is amplified through the trumpet so that everyone in the room can hear the message, regardless of who is being addressed. Balls or hoops with fluorescent markers on them can also be used. As they move around the room, going in any and all directions, all sitters can see their movements at the same time. This type of demonstration is a marvelous one to witness.

## Direct voice box

Here, Spirit uses the medium's energy to form an ectoplasmic voice box to communicate with the sitters in the room. Often the Spirit voice will start out quite inaudible, garbled or unintelligible. As the energy builds up, the Spirit person will be able to communicate quite clearly for all in the room to hear. Men, women and children of all nationalities and races are able to speak, even if the medium is not proficient in any of the languages, dialects or accents that are spoken. This type of communication requires a tremendous amount of energy to achieve and is always conducted while sitting in the dark.

## Ouija

Otherwise known as a Spirit Board, the Ouija is used to communicate with Spirit during a séance. The board typically has words, letters and numbers printed on it that Spirit would use to communicate with the sitters. Everyone in attendance will usually lightly place a fingertip on the *planchette*, a heart-shaped device with a pointer that will indicate which letter, word or number is being referenced.

Through the Ouija Board, Spirit will spell out names and provide dates of birth or street addresses for those present, as well as valuable messages. Although it is a wonderful experience to behold, it can be laborious and time-consuming for the participants and the Spirit communicator alike.

There has been a great deal of misuse and misrepresentation of the Ouija Board throughout the ages, and Hollywood has certainly added to the fear surrounding it. In my experience, it can be a highly beneficial and irrefutable communication tool. It needs to be used, however, with the three Rs of mediumship: *respect, reverence and responsibility.*

Using it as an entertainment device, or while under the influence of alcohol, or as a toy, is disrespectful and an insult to the Spirit world. Demanding Spirit speak through it, as is often depicted in paranormal

TV programs, shows a complete lack of respect and understanding of the purpose of the board and, more importantly, of the Spirit contact.

## Levitation

Spirit may physically levitate some mediums whilst sitting in their chairs in an séance. This is a very powerful demonstration of Spirit's presence and occurs with no visible means of support whatsoever. As mentioned before, this may also occur with solid objects brought into the séance for that purpose. Levitation is a rare skill and infrequently witnessed in modern times.

## Spirit lights or orbs

These orbs or balls of light, usually white, yellow or red in color, are representations of Spirit. Some discernment is required when viewing orbs as not all orbs are Spirit – some are just dust swirling about the room! Orbs will usually move quickly and in many directions. They respond to human communication with intelligence, and generate emotions of awe and wellbeing in those who witness them.

## Apports

During a séance, Spirit will at times materialize out of thin air objects that are referred to as *apports*. These apported objects may be anything from coins, feathers, jewelry, flowers or any other item that usually has some significance for the recipient.

An apported coin, for example, may have been minted in the birth year of the recipient's loved one in Spirit. If the materialized object is organic in nature, such as a flower, its life span will be longer than normal due to the high level of vibration that was infused into it by the Spirit team.

I once had an experience where I told a client that his mother would come to him as a large red and black butterfly. At first, he couldn't relate to the message, but later that year, while at the funeral of his sister, a butterfly matching this exact description landed on his shoulder and remained there for a long period of time. This was in the midst of a deep, snowy winter, when there were definitely no butterflies in the area. This is also considered a type of apport, since a living thing from a faraway location was brought to the man's location.

Another time, I was in the middle of giving a direct voice reading (where the Spirit person speaks directly through me to my sitter). I was holding my client's hand while wearing my favorite ring when suddenly I felt my ring disappear from my hand; it had simply vanished into thin air. I knew the client hadn't removed it from my hand, yet my logical mind wanted to accuse him of taking my ring. I heard a laugh from Spirit, and the sitter informed me that his grandmother loved jewelry, especially rings. His grandmother in the Spirit world had decided to *borrow* my ring for the day. I was bewildered, to say the least, but felt certain that it would be returned. Sure enough, a day later I found that my ring had been returned and placed in my make-up case – a place I would never leave jewelry. In this case, the apport was taken from me and put in another location at a later time.

Physical mediumship is quite controversial and requires extensive preparation. If you're drawn to this field of work, I suggest you attend a few physical mediumship demonstrations and witness for yourself what happens. Alternatively, find a reputable and ethical closed circle with a developing physical medium to help you make up your mind. Most importantly, use your discernment to be certain that Spirit is there. It is very easy to get carried away by the emotional release of other people and to believe you've actually seen or felt Spirit when you have not. Test the medium and test Spirit; ask for confirmation that is irrefutable for you.

An example of receiving evidential confirmation occurred when I attended an séance with British medium Gordon Garforth. It was the first time I would sit in the dark with a red light and witness such an event, and I went with an open, yet questioning, mind. While driving to the venue, I was chatting to my beloved grandmother in Spirit, and I asked her to help me determine the legitimacy of this medium. I requested that she materialize and for the medium to speak in my grandmother's native tongue, Greek.

You can imagine my delight when my grandmother was the first face that transfigured (appeared over the medium's face via ectoplasm) and proceeded to perform a mannerism that confirmed beyond a shadow of a doubt that it was she who was present! Her energy filled the room and I was delighted to receive a physical embrace from her as well. Later that same evening, my dear grandfather's features transfigured over the face of this medium and I heard Greek being spoken. This was my second confirmation delivered as I had requested, although admittedly the medium struggled with the Greek words, as it was not his native tongue. I was very grateful to have witnessed such a demonstration and because I received such clear confirmation, I can highly recommend Gordon Garforth as a legitimate and skilled physical medium.

As you can see, genuine physical mediums do exist and have much to offer in a reading; I sincerely hope you have the good fortune to experience one. However, as stated before, it is important to use discretion in choosing whom to trust. To counteract fraud, it has been suggested that physical mediums lead their circles under low-level red light and that infrared cameras be present. This has caused a division in the mediumistic community, as many mediums claim that actual physical harm can be done to a medium if exposed to any kind of light when they're working, due to the level of energy involved.

As a person with an engineering background, I look forward to the day where technology and Spirit work together to produce spectacular results. I'm a firm believer that as more and more people of many professions – including scientists, mediums and physicists – cross into the world of Spirit and reach out to make their knowledge known, this area of mediumship will continue to grow, adapt and change. As our knowledge and understanding grows and more and more double-blind experiments are conducted, then hopefully irrefutable evidence of phenomena will be witnessed, recorded and accepted.

I certainly don't claim to have all the answers to this contentious topic but I do believe further and more rigorous testing needs to be completed in a supportive and non-judgmental way. We need to be prepared that the medium and the Spirit team may fail many times, but when they do get it right, it will be truly amazing to witness. The same holds true in other fields such as science, where thousands of experimental hours are accrued before success is reported.

## Trance mediumship

Trance mediumship technically is a form of mental mediumship and may be broken down into three subcategories; *trance healing, trance communication* and *trance speaking*. In some parts of the world this form of mediumship is commonly referred to as *channeling*.

Before I explore the three areas of trance mediumship I wish to clarify the meaning of the word *trance*. People often believe that trance involves mediums going into an entranced state where we are unable to control ourselves, or that Spirit enters and takes over our bodies. This is not the case, and in fact most of us will have gone into a trance state daily without even knowing it.

If you've ever been driving a car and reached your destination without really being aware of how you got there, chances are that you were in a light trance state. Similarly, you are effectively going into trance when you go through the process of going to sleep or waking up. Perhaps the most common instance where people go into trance is when they're watching television; this is commonly referred to as *zoning out*. Any activity that you are performing in automatic mode, without being consciously aware, is done in a light trance state.

The techniques used to get into the trance state are similar to those employed by hypnotherapists. Some type of induction process is usually employed. This may be as simple as a self-induction where you count backwards slowly, yet rhythmically, from a high number to zero in your mind to achieve a trance state. Alternatively, others may use music such as rhythmic drumming to achieve this state.

In trance mediumship, your attention is taken away from what you're doing, and this happens through Spirit. In other words, you're often not aware of your immediate environment or your thoughts; this awareness still exists but it becomes less relevant. It's as if the volume switch of your mind is turned down. In fact, the worst thing that could happen in the trance state is that you might actually fall asleep!

Any experience that is uncomfortable is merely your own mental mind clearing out the subconscious mind. We experience discomfort when we're trying to control the process of going into trance, or when we've allowed fear to grip us. Spirit will not make the trance process uncomfortable.

Your state of mind will determine what type of trance experience you have. If you are in a loving state of mind, you will attract a loving type of Spirit. If you perceive trance to be scary, then your experience will reflect this. Hollywood has a lot to answer for, as Spirit possession is usually portrayed to induce fear in the viewer.

It is not unusual when developing mediums are first starting to experiment with trance for them to report that they felt sensations that were like cobwebs on their faces. This is not Spirit touching their face; rather, it is a physiological reaction that occurs when their consciousness changes state.

There are many levels of awareness or trance states that can be experienced and developed over time. The levels may be broadly grouped into four categories: hypnoidal, light trance, medium trance and deep trance. A novice medium may start off at the light level and utilize either speaking or writing. With consistent development, they may be able to achieve deep trance states, like Edgar Cayce, who was famously referred to as *the sleeping prophet*. It's important to remember that achieving such a deep trance state takes many hours of practice, very much like working out at a gym. You wouldn't expect to go to a gym and instantly lift the heaviest weights there; rather, you'd start out with lighter weights and gradually build up over time.

The four levels of trance states are described below, but it is not necessary to know which state you are in to experience them.

- **Hypnoidal trance** – you progress from ordinary consciousness through each of the following steps: you feel physically relaxed and drowsy as your mind becomes relaxed. You may feel apathetic or indifferent. Your arms and legs start to feel heavy. You may have a tendency to stare blankly and a disinclination to move your limbs. As you reach the border between this and the state known as light trance your breathing becomes slower and deeper, and your pulse rate slows.

- **Light trance** – you progress to a reluctance to move, speak, think or act. You may experience some involuntary twitching of your mouth or jaw, and sometimes of the eyes. You will feel heaviness throughout your entire body and a partial feeling of detachment. You may also experience visual images through your clairvoyance. As you enter the border between this and the medium trance state, you recognize that you are in a trance, but may find that feeling hard to describe.

- **Medium trance** – you definitely recognize that you're in a trance state and may experience partial amnesia unless you consciously choose not to. You can experience the psychic senses of touch, taste and smell. You'll be more sensitive to variations in atmospheric pressure and temperature changes. At the border of this and the deep trance state you may experience complete catalepsy of your limbs or body. In other words, if your limbs or body positions are changed you will leave them in the new position until they are changed again.

- **Deep trance** – you may have the ability to open your eyes without affecting the trance. You'll also have the ability to control such body functions as heartbeat, blood pressure, digestion, and body temperature. You can make your body and limbs completely rigid. You'll be able to recall lost memories and experience age regression. Here you can experience the sensation of lightness, floating, or flying and being outside the constraints of time.

## Trance writing

During trance, one may experience what is known as inspirational writing or trance writing. In fact, trance writing is how I was first introduced to Spirit teachings. I recall in my early years of development, because I lacked understanding of trance and was fearful of being taken over; I seemed to miss my classes when inspirational writing was being practiced. I believe this was an unconscious avoidance, as we never knew from week to week what our topic of development would be.

Interestingly in 2008, when I ran my first development circle, I had never experienced inspirational writing myself. Thinking I was being very clever I set my students up with the task of doing inspirational writing and was reassuring them that it was safe and there was nothing to be fearful of. I was thinking it was great that I could teach it but didn't have to do it myself. Sure enough, I heard a voice very clearly say to me, 'You will be writing messages for all your students while they're doing their writing'. My trust in Spirit was rock solid, so I pulled out pen and paper and allowed Spirit to write through me.

I wrote so much that my shoulder, wrist and fingers ached, but at the completion of the exercise the unexpressed fear I'd had had been dissolved. Ironically, I now employ this method to obtain clear answers to any question I may have, and I love it!

## Trance healing

*'In Spirit healing the intelligent direction of a healing or other*
*force originates from the Spirit realm.'*
*~ Harry Edwards*

This quote from the acclaimed Spiritual healer and medium Harry Edwards very succinctly defines what Spirit or trance healing is about. For me trance or Spirit healing is a beautiful form of mediumship where the medium will facilitate a healing directed from the Spirit world. With this type of mediumship you can literally assist thousands of people at any given time. Spirit healing transcends time and space; it is not even necessary for the medium to know or have a personal connection with the receiver.

It is the ultimate form of service and is done without expectation of an outcome, whether facilitating it either in person or remotely, as is the case in *distant healing*. In absent or distant healing Spirit can identify the root cause of the issue and send the appropriate healing energy or force to a recipient located anywhere in the world.

It is important to note that the word 'healing' does not imply curing, although in some cases we have seen just that. Personal responsibility is a must for any type of healing to be effective; if a traditional doctor prescribes you effective medication and you fail to take it, then you cannot expect to become well. The same can be said for Spirit healing: if a message is passed on about the root cause of the issue and you fail to respond to that, then you'll continue to experience your ailment.

In my personal experience I have found consistently that the adage 'as above, so below' applies in my healing work. Every health care professional or expert, both in traditional and complementary medicine, that has ever existed on Earth may be found and utilized in the Spirit world.

From a practical level, it's much better to get out of the way and let the Spirit doctors and healers direct the healing energies. They will have far superior insights regarding the root cause of an illness and the healing given will be truly holistic in nature: mind, body and Spirit will all be worked upon.

The worst thing you can do is actually asking the person seeking a healing what's wrong. This immediately engages the active conscious mind that will try to problem-solve based on its limited knowledge and perceptions.

So how does one go about giving a trance healing to a recipient? The mechanics will vary according to personal preference. Some will have the recipient sitting in a chair and others will use a professional massage or healing table, where the recipient is lying down. Please note that the recipient is always fully clothed, since Spiritual healing, being vibrational in nature, is not impeded by clothing, furniture, plaster casts, etc.

Some mediums or trance healers will place their hands directly on the recipient's shoulders or body, while others will be strictly hands-off. Consider a position that will be comfortable for you, as you may be in trance for a long period of time. I personally prefer hands-on and will cradle the head or hold the shoulders of my recipient while they are lying down.

It's my belief that touch in itself can be healing and reassuring for the recipient; however, I'm mindful that some people don't like to be touched, and always check with my recipient. No healing, be it in person or via distance, should be initiated without prior permission and agreement being given to the Medium by the recipient.

Of course, the beauty of being a trance healer is that the medium as a healing channel will also benefit from the healing energies they're channeling. It's not uncommon for the healing medium to report feeling energized after the healing session is completed. Once again, intention is key; you must have the intention of becoming a healing channel to avoid becoming a magnetic healer. A magnetic healer will use his or her own energy to blend with the recipient's and thus become depleted, drained and tired after the session. When *channeling* healing, you will be left feeling energized.

In some healing circles you may hear the term *psychic surgery* used; in trance healing, however, no physical surgery is being undertaken. It is merely a process of energy thought that takes place. When the Spirit doctors that heal through me undertake psychic surgery I'm shown in my mind's eye gloved surgeon's hands and sterilized medical equipment being unwrapped ready to be used. This is a visual indicator or signal that lets me know what's about to happen.

The first time Spirit doctors started working through me was quite a memorable experience. I was using reiki techniques with a female client when all of a sudden I saw through my clairvoyance large surgeon's hands appear in front of me, blending with my own hands. I then saw a scalpel being used and an energetic incision being made in the woman's abdomen. I saw a mass being cut out and then dropped into a metal bowl on the floor at my feet. The wound was then cauterized and the woman sewn back up. Of course, this was witnessed through my psychic senses rather than my physical eyes. I even heard through my clairaudience the sound of the removed mass hitting the metallic bowl.

I knew in that moment that that woman had been cured of a cancer in her energetic body that would have been actualized in her physical body if she had not sought out healing.

Since that initial healing I've been privileged to witness countless miraculous healings that have encompassed fertility, loss of eyesight, chronic illness and even motor neuron disease, to name but a few. Each one has been extraordinary, and what I've learnt is that generally there is a deep unprocessed emotion that is the root cause of most ailments that manifest in the body. This emotion may be rooted in adulthood, childhood, in utero, pre-conception, or even in a past life.

The healing work has been most rewarding for me as it has had a direct impact on people and their lives. I've had countless people say that they were suicidal until they met me and they have healed and gone on to live full and meaningful lives. This has been very humbling for me, as I know that so many people suffer in silence and don't realize that there is a whole team of loving benevolent beings waiting to heal them.

One of my most memorable examples of Spiritual healing occurred with my own grandfather. He was diagnosed with mouth cancer in his seventies, and the consulting physician refused to work on him, saying that he would not survive the surgery. He was advised to live out his remaining days as best he could. Seeking a second opinion, he found a surgeon who was willing to work on him, but he also relayed the high risk of this particular kind of surgery. The night before his surgery, as my grandfather lay in bed feeling very apprehensive, he was visited by an Asian doctor who told him that he would be working on him the next morning and not to worry, for all would be well.

The next day, he was wheeled into surgery feeling calmer and more hopeful, though still a little nervous. His procedure was a success, and when his surgeon visited him back on the ward later that day my grandfather asked if he could speak to the Asian doctor who had worked on him. The surgeon looked bemused and told him that there were no Asian doctors on staff at all in the Greek hospital. I have no doubt that a Spirit doctor had visited my grandfather to let him know he'd be working on him alongside the other doctors throughout his surgery.

Another example of Spirit doctors being present and providing healing occurred with my own father, who was a born skeptic and non-believer of Spirit. One year, my father received his annual flu vaccine along with the swine flu vaccine, and within hours he suffered a reaction that rendered him unable to walk. He was placed in hospital while a barrage of tests was conducted to determine what had happened. Four weeks went by with no improvement to his condition. At his lowest point, he thought to himself, 'I would rather be dead than not able to walk again.' In the early hours of the morning, he was awoken by a knock on his head and heard a voice commanding him to get up now and he would be able to walk again. Remarkably, my father got up and attempted to walk and to his surprise was able to take a number of steps. The next morning, my father told his doctor that he had walked the night before. The doctor was skeptical, saying this was impossible; he asked my father to prove it to him. My father stood up and walked again! The doctor was at a loss as to how this had happened, and could only say, 'Whatever you're doing – keep doing it!'

I have no doubt that these and many other examples are the work of a loving healing energy that is greater than we can understand. Spirit helpers from the other side were motivated to help and provide healing to my grandfather and to my father in these two examples. The love that Spirit has for us is a motivating and healing force that can, in some instances, produce miraculous results. At other times, it is able to provide comfort and peace when there is no physical hope.

### Trance communication/Trance speaking

The aim of *trance communication* is to introduce an intelligence or wisdom from the Spirit world for the purposes of bringing about enlightenment, illumination or knowledge. The demonstrating medium will blend with a Spirit being who is enlightened or was known for their teachings or knowledge specialty, and that Spirit person will then address an attending audience. The Spirit person has the capacity to interact with the audience, answering questions and having knowledge or information that is specific to the enquirer. The demonstrating medium will usually employ an assistant to transcribe the information given, since the medium will usually not have full conscious awareness of what is being said.

These Spirit beings are known collectively as *Inspirers* and can represent all walks of life; they don't necessarily have to be well-known identities such as Einstein or Plato, for instance, although it's not unusual for well-known identities to decide to speak. More often than not, it's the medium's main guide who tends to speak, talking about their take on life and answering questions based on their own perspective and experiences.

As you commence your trance speaking development, you may find that as these Inspirers are speaking through you in the trance state you may come out of trance if what is being said is something you don't believe in or agree with. The most difficult part about trance speaking is relinquishing control and letting yourself wholly surrender to Spirit.

Over time and with consistent practice, you'll train your mind not to get involved so that you may function as a pure conduit of communication. You'll be able to go into trance more deeply and therefore not interfere with what's being conveyed. The more passive you become, the purer a channel you become, so try not to get involved with the impressions and descriptors you get from the Spirit person who has blended with you. This will be counterproductive, since your active conscious mind will tend to interact with the information and thus pull you out of the trance state.

In *trance speaking*, however, the medium actually embodies the personalities of loved ones from the world of Spirit who use the medium to communicate with their living family members. The sitter will witness a change in personality of the medium and be able to recognize their loved one from the Spirit world based on their defining mannerisms, vocabulary and spoken details relating to their lives.

The most difficult part of trance speaking or trance communication is relinquishing control, surrendering to Spirit and allowing Spirit to speak. On a practical level it is important to keep your head upright so that if you do speak your audience or sitters can hear what you have to say. In addition, ensure that you're seated comfortably and supported so that bodily discomfort doesn't bring you out of the trance state.

When going into trance there are various physical symptoms that you may experience, from rapid eye movement to jerking of the body. Your mouth may either go very dry or be full of saliva. These symptoms are all perfectly normal and should not be feared by either the medium or those observing the medium.

In some instances, you may also experience a natural chemical and emotional release resulting in tears as you are speaking or after you have come out of trance. Alternatively, you may tremble, become nauseous or feel very cold; again, this is perfectly normal.

In the trance state you may feel your body as being much larger or smaller than you are. Just remain passive and go with this; try not to be too curious, as you will engage your conscious mind and come out of trance. Simply be an observer.

After a deep trance experience, some mediums may be very sensitive to noise and light. Often they require the assistance of a helper, who will ensure they're able to walk without feeling dizzy. The medium may need to re-attune themselves to everyday life. This can take up to twenty minutes, or more in some cases.

## Trance induction methods

There are three types of trance induction process: the counting method, the Spirit method and the drumming method. It's useful to set an intention before you employ any of these methods, for example: 'as I practice these exercises I will go deeper and deeper into the trance state. Although I am going into the trance state, I will remain aware of everything that I say and do. When I return to normal consciousness, I will remember clearly and completely everything that I have experienced.' This intention will counter any tendency to fall asleep when starting to practice these induction processes.

### Counting method

- Sit quietly and comfortably in a chair (don't lie down as you're likely to fall asleep), somewhere you won't be disturbed. Ensure any distractions and noises are minimized and your phones are switched off.

- Set the intention that Spirit will blend with you. In your mind start counting down slowly from a large arbitrary number such as 500 in a monotonic voice. First focus on slowing your breathing, then pause before focusing on breathing in from the solar plexus. Keep counting down backwards slowly until you feel the presence of Spirit.

- Practice this process without any expectation other than sitting in the trance state. If you feel yourself coming out of trance before your practice time is up, just begin counting again from the last number you recall. Once you have sat in trance for a predefined time, invite Spirit to step away from you, and then count yourself back to full awareness slowly, to prevent a feeling of nausea occurring. Over time you'll learn what pace of counting best suits you and your body as you come out of trance. Do not place any pressure on yourself to speak; allow that to happen naturally when you become sufficiently attuned over time.

*Spirit method*

- Sit quietly and comfortably in chair (don't lie down as you're likely to fall asleep), somewhere you're not likely to be disturbed. Ensure any distractions and noises are minimized and your phones are switched off. Set the intention that you're going to blend with Spirit, then repeatedly state in your mind: 'Here I am, take me into the trance, here I am, take me into the trance ...'. State this slowly and rhythmically until you feel the presence of Spirit blending with you.

- Sit in this passive state until you're ready to return, either at a predefined time, by setting a timer, or by setting the intention that you'll sit for a certain period of time and then allowing Spirit to bring you back out of trance. If you're using a timer, choose an alarm tone that's soft and gentle, so that you're not startled out of trance.

*Drumming method*

- Listen to music that's created for the purposes of inducing a trance state, or alternatively practice shamanic drumming and bring yourself into trance via the drumming process.
- Shamanic drumming uses a repetitive rhythm that begins slowly and then gradually builds in intensity to a tempo of three to seven beats per second. The ascending tempo induces a light to deep trance state. When you're ready to exit the trance state, simply slow the tempo of drumming down while you return to normal consciousness. Shamanic drumming has been used in many tribal cultures around the world, both in ancient and modern times. It continues to offer today what it has offered for thousands of years: namely, a simple and effective technique of achieving a trance state.
- When using the drums, be careful if you have heart issues as the drums can disrupt the heart energy. Don't listen to the music as a piece of music but rather focus on the sound vibration that creates a change of energy within and around you.

As you can see, there are many styles of mediumship and you may already be naturally developed in some of them. I would encourage you to explore these styles under the expert guidance of a mentor who will be able to assess your suitability for each style of mediumship. Remember: just because we're attracted to a particular style does not automatically mean that we have the capacity to work in that way. You may have hidden ability in a style that you might not have considered before and this too may be uncovered with the assistance of a skilled mentor.

**Exercises**

1. Spirit utilizes a medium's accumulated knowledge, life experiences, abilities, teachings, readings, and fields of study, both formal and informal. All these experiences we've had are effectively like a giant storage container or filing cabinet that Spirit dips into to retrieve information to convey messages to us. To strengthen and deepen your mediumship, strive to continuously educate yourself. Read; learn; experience. Learn another language or branch out into a creative field. In short, be curious, open, daring and courageous! Any additional knowledge increases the size of the filing cabinet and therefore your reach widens and your accuracy improves.

2. Keep an inspirational writing journal where you write questions at the top of the page. Allow yourself to go into a light trance state and then allow your soul's wisdom to speak to you through the use of the hand holding the pen. Once you've paused, and the writing no longer flows, this is the time to stop. If you find yourself having to pause and think, then know that you've engaged your conscious mind rather than your inspired Spirit.

3. Practice going into trance using one of the three induction methods discussed in this chapter. Determine which method you're more attuned to. Development of deep breathing techniques is a must for every method.

4. Go into trance and send distance healing to people in need, including to the ones who challenge you or who have hurt you the most. Do this without any expectation of resolution or outcome.

5. Use your clairvoyance to see the headstone at the gravesite or an inscription at the memorial of a Spirit person and describe that to your sitter.

6. Use your clairaudience to hear a sound associated with a hobby connected to the Spirit person and describe that to your sitter.

7. Use your clairsentience to feel the physical appearance of the Spirit person. Did their physical presence change due to illness? Describe this to your sitter.

8. Use your clairgustance to receive a taste that is significant to the Spirit person such as favorite food or tobacco. Describe this to your sitter.

9. Form your own physical mediumship circle with nine trusted sitters who are dedicated and committed to being part of a process that may take years to develop and get results. Make the time to sit regularly, without any expectations. Let your Spirit team guide you.

CHAPTER 5

# Opening your mediumship

*'When you are with Spirit, there is no need to worry'*
*~ Gordon Higginson*

A ll mediums are naturally developed to a certain degree since their soul is already equipped with all the development tools, skills and knowledge necessary for mediumship to unfold. All that remains for the developing medium is to find a way to illuminate their pathway; to shed light on the next steps of their development.

This is where the skills of a competent mentor come into play. Under the guidance of a skilled mentor who is trained to ignite the medium's soul by instilling confidence, trust and assurance, the medium is able to expand to a far deeper level than self-practice alone can provide.

From the moment someone becomes consciously aware that they're a medium, a drive or urgency presents within them to open and develop this ability further. At this time, they're in their most vulnerable state as they try to absorb and assimilate techniques, skills and methods of working with Spirit. They're vulnerable simply because their foundational skill set is not yet solid. As a result, they'll tend to look outside of themselves and compare themselves to others, forgetting that even the most accomplished mediums were also beginners once.

Sometimes naturally developed mediums discount or negate their ability because they don't actually *see* Spirit. When I meet mediums who feel this way, I try to educate them that sight is only one of the psychic faculties that mediums employ; not seeing Spirit doesn't lessen their ability. It is clairsentience, or the *feeling* of Spirit, which I place a greater value on, for when we feel we can truly empath, and it is empathy that drives healing.

To truly understand the mechanics of mediumship we must first understand that it is the *soul* that initiates a connection with Spirit. Then the medium draws Spirit close through their *thoughts*. It is through this understanding that Spiritualists have coined the phrase, 'from soul, through soul, to soul'. This sums up quite succinctly for me the essence of mediumship.

The Spirit world wishes you to communicate on their behalf and consequently will utilize all the experiences and knowledge you've had that are *unique to you*, sifting through them as if they were housed in a filing cabinet in your mind. Your job as a medium is to pass through the signs and information that Spirit gives you without coloring it with your own interpretation or logic. In other words, give it as you get it.

Mind mastery therefore is a must when working mediumistically so that you're able to work with Spirit in as pure a state as possible. A 100 per cent clear communication channel is never achieved, because the conscious mind will always interfere with the thought stream; however, minimizing the interference of the conscious mind is key to developing your mediumship to a competent level. A competent medium trusts what they're given and will pass it through without interpretation, even if it doesn't seem logical to them.

As I've mentioned, mediumship development is not a one-size-fits-all process. My recommendation is that you experiment with various techniques and use those that resonate best with you. Use every spare moment to practice techniques, and experiment with your mediumship in a practice circle or under the guidance of a mentor.

You will already have a natural style or ability but it is the deeper, stronger techniques combined with discipline and practice that separate a mediocre medium from an accomplished one. When witnessing an excellent medium demonstrate publicly, you can be assured that behind them are countless hours and often years of practice. I cannot emphasize this enough: excellent quality of mediumship is achieved with dedication, persistence and, above all, the desire to serve humanity as the prime motivator.

Countless exercises and techniques exist to help you open yourself up, allowing your mediumship to flourish. In the exercises at the end of this chapter, you'll find some of the techniques I've successfully employed with my students. You may wish to experiment with these techniques and see which are suitable for you.

Be *you*! Be unique and allow the Spirit world to determine how they wish to work with you, based on your own unique set of experiences. A conscious, motivated and disciplined mind, combined with regular practice, will deepen your mediumship ability. Don't expect to progress your mediumship by taking a weekend course or a two-hour class each term. You must be motivated and inspired to continuously develop until the day comes for you, too, to make the transition into the Spirit world.

Above all, you need to trust, and be prepared to make mistakes. If you can understand that at times in your development you may be wrong, and remain humble and open to refining your techniques, then you'll be a stronger medium for it. Always go back to your Spirit team and seek their guidance as to how you can improve for next time.

In the following section I've outlined some areas of development that I recommend for you, to further open your mediumship on a more holistic level. In other words, mediumship development is not just about learning the mechanics of mediumship but also about developing yourself as a person and a soul.

# Understanding you

Getting to know yourself will enhance your mediumship. Self-mastery through self-awareness is key. Understand who you are and what makes you tick. Look within yourself and find your source of power: what motivates you, what engages you, what drives you. Your power may be found where your *passion* is; by tapping into your passion you're building your personal power. Understand your strengths and weaknesses, and be comfortable with who you are. Be true to your soul, your soul's blueprint and your own unique DNA. In other words, trust that your soul knows what to do and then get out of your own way.

By trying to emulate or mimic others, you do yourself and your mediumship development a disservice. Know that your own unique mediumship blueprint is *already encoded and contained in your soul.* Never lose your own individuality and personality. Rather, use your uniqueness as your calling card – the thing that differentiates you from other mediums. Remember, there are as many kinds of sitters as there are mediums. Spirit knows which medium to send their sitter to, based on the personal qualities needed. For this reason, I say again: stay true to yourself, for by doing so you're staying true to Spirit.

Develop and cultivate faith, trust and belief in yourself. Never forget that when you make a contact with the Spirit world, there actually is someone on the Other Side who is touched by that contact. That someone is a real being with a personality; with likes, dislikes, and defining characteristics that are unique to them. We can sometimes become so focused on our mediumship process and on the sitter before us that we forget this amazing and wonderful fact. Keep in mind that as much is happening on the Other Side as is happening on this side; the ripple effect occurs in all directions.

Make a regular appointment to sit with your Spirit team to grow in your understanding of your path and how you can best serve Spirit and all of humanity. Remember, this is a two-way conversation; it's not always about sitting passively waiting for instructions or guidance. You're an ambassador for the Spirit world, and as such your aim is to develop a relationship dialogue, a two-way conversation, about how you can best serve.

Take the time to understand your own life and energy cycles so that you work with your natural rhythm rather than against it. Throughout the year, you may find that your energy peaks in a particular season – during summer, for example – and therefore you may be most suited at that time to public work, which requires a higher energy load. In other times, when your energy is more passive, you might take up trance healing or trance communication work.

At particular stages in your life you may find that your mediumship changes, allowing you to move into areas of mediumship that you would not have considered in the past. This happened to me when I moved into the public demonstrating arena. If you'd asked me years earlier whether I would take the platform and demonstrate, you'd have received a resounding 'No!' Today, of course, Spirit has influenced me to become more active in public demonstrating. As a result, I now run a monthly gathering called Meraki Spiritualist Society, where, together with my students in Melbourne, Australia, I demonstrate mediumship publicly and offer healing and inspiration. The name 'Meraki' reflects my Greek heritage and means to do something with *soul, creativity, and love.*

## Mastering the psychic senses

The cornerstone of mediumship development is the mastery of the psychic senses. The art of mediumship is like a multifaceted diamond where each facet represents one of the psychic senses: clairvoyance, clairaudience, claircognizance, clairsentience, clairsalience, and clairgustance.

All the psychic senses must be embraced to fully utilize all the information Spirit makes available for us during a mediumship reading. Every piece of evidence made available by Spirit brings with it a unique brilliance that may be appreciated by the sitter. A reading will contain many layers of simultaneous information that embrace sight, sound, smell, taste and feeling.

A skilled medium will move beyond the obvious information and search deeper for the hidden gems that present in a multi-faceted communication stream. For example, you may see a silver stopwatch in your hand with your clairvoyance; at this point, you have the option of merely passing this on as fact to the recipient, or you may choose to go deeper. This one piece of information may have a wealth of further detail associated with it, if you're willing to look for it. How does the watch feel to you in your hand? Is it well worn from being held many times? Turn it over to observe if there are any significant markings, initials or design on it? Where is the watch now? How was the watch acquired? Was it buried with the owner or passed on to someone living?

As you can see, one piece of evidence has now deepened into many layers of evidence. By using several of the available psychic senses we're able to build up a stronger evidential picture than what's possible with one simple fact.

We're all born with at least one and often many more of these senses already naturally developed and available for us to use. The clue to which of these senses is naturally developed within you lies in the language you use in your ordinary day-to-day speech. If you find yourself saying, 'My feeling on this is …' or other emotive phrases such as 'I love …', then know you're naturally *clairsentient*. Similarly, if you find yourself saying, 'I see your point …', then you're most likely a visual person and therefore your *clairvoyance* is naturally dominant. This holds true for all of the other psychic clairs.

Don't be discouraged from developing the other non-dominant clairs just because you're not naturally developed in those areas. With a little patience and practice you'll progress and develop skills that encompass all the clairs. Doing so will improve and widen your ability to communicate with Spirit and with others from all walks of life.

How do we strengthen our psychic muscle? The answer to this is to practice, both formally through classes and exercises and informally by undertaking any activity that activates the creativity center in your brain. Take up a new creative pursuit and challenge yourself by moving beyond your comfort zone. Join a dance class, enroll in an art class or simply design a new garden. Creative pursuits stimulate the right side of your brain, which governs your intuition. By doing activities and tasks that are right-brain focused you're automatically working on your psychic skills.

In my household when I was growing up there was a running joke around the telephone ringing. When it rang, the household would pause, all eyes would be on me and they'd say 'Who's calling?' I'd tune in and state a name and be delighted when whoever answered the phone confirmed the name I'd given. Other times I'd watch quiz shows and try to guess answers that I didn't already know. I noticed over time that when I was drawn to an answer, it was always right. If I second-guessed myself or rethought the answer, I was always wrong.

This type of practice was like a game to me so I was able to develop in an environment that was supportive and nurturing. There are many other ways of doing this, such as picking the color of the next playing card drawn from a deck. (Note, there is a difference between guessing and consciously tuning in. To tune in, focus your energy on the card and try to perceive the color that comes to mind.) The main point I'm making is to have fun with it as you're refining and honing your ability. Be kind to yourself while being persistent with your practice.

A formal way to build and exercise your psychic muscle is by joining a psychic development class and sitting in regular practice. In this environment, under the mentorship of a skilled group leader, you'll gain understanding of your dominant clairs. Practice, through the undertaking of specific exercises, will strengthen your non-dominant clairs and further enhance your dominant ones.

It is my firm belief that all mediumship development must start with psychic development. Psychic senses are our birthright and a great tool to master for life in general and in your mediumship. Trusting and strengthening your abilities will allow you to accelerate your development since you won't be second-guessing yourself and the information you perceive.

*Building your personal power* on a practical level will allow you to open and further strengthen your mediumship. Any activity that you undertake to build this power within you will serve you well when working with Spirit. What do I mean by personal power? I mean that energy that motivates you into action, fueled by your passion. It is the life force energy that is present in us all and that moves the Spirit within us, allowing for the full expression of our soul.

Ways to build our personal power include activities based on our interests that increase your chi or life force energy. For some it might be as simple as undertaking a regular meditation practice, while for others it may be yoga, tai chi, qi gong or breath work. If you make time to pursue your passions and do so regularly, your personal power will be fueled, lifting it to a higher frequency and rate. If you've ever been in the presence of someone who's speaking from their heart about a topic they're passionate about, you may have found that you too were inspired, as if their passion and enthusiasm were contagious.

*Regular self-care* is essential; rest when you feel tired and engage in self-care practices such as simple walks or a regular massage, reiki or healing. Become very self-aware so that you understand your energy and its patterns and how seasons, situations and environments affect it. By working with your own arcadian rhythms, rather than against them, you'll use your energy stores efficiently and wisely. (See Chapter 11, 'The importance of self-care', for more detailed information.)

The most important practice, however, is to take the time to *sit in the power with your Spirit team.* Find a time when you won't be disturbed and make a regular appointment to sit with your Spirit guides. Connect to ground and pull up the energy, activating each chakra with the *intention* that you are connecting with your team. (See exercise 2 at the end of Chapter 7, 'Mediumship skills and tools', for a full description of how to do this.) Get to know your team intimately and find out how they wish to work with you and what you need to do to facilitate and improve this process.

Remember: it is a *dialogue*, not a monologue. Imagine if you made an appointment to meet with an adviser – a financial adviser, for example – and once you arrived you sat there without speaking or communicating with them. No doubt you'd leave feeling disappointment about the fact that no communication had occurred. Most people sit in the power and expect their guides to download information without them even initiating a connection! *Intention* is key.

## Embrace the noes

One of the best ways to open your mediumship involves ironically the one thing mediums fear the most, and that is the word 'no'. When we're giving a reading, particularly in a public forum, we get energized when we hear a 'yes' from our recipient. We're delighted to receive a confirmation and become far more ignited in our power.

The 'no', however, fills us with dread and quite often may result in us losing our power and dropping our connection with Spirit. There's nothing worse as a developing medium than giving evidence and hearing nothing but the sound of crickets as you wait desperately for someone to take the evidence given.

I recall during a demonstration I gave in Scotland that my first contact of the evening was given and no one could take the evidence. I kept persisting with more specific and detailed information, and still no one could take the evidence. As I zeroed in on my recipient she kept staring at me with a blank face, not responding with an affirmative. At this point I had an internal moment of dread, but I positively knew I had Spirit with me so on behalf of my Spirit person I rallied my energy and power. I went back to my recipient and said I knew without a doubt that I was with her and asked her which of the evidence I had given she could not understand. She stated that she could accept all the information I gave. In this case, she had become so overwhelmed by the specifics that she was dumbfounded. Later I found out it was her first time at such a demonstration and she had come in with a very skeptical mind. She was quite shocked by the quality of the evidence given.

This reinforced for me that getting a 'no' response may in fact not mean that you as a medium have the evidence wrong; it may be that the person it relates to is unable to respond in that moment. There's a term that we use when this happens: *psychic amnesia*. It's not uncommon for a recipient to be driving home after the event, for instance, and suddenly be able to place the evidence that you gave.

For me, the difference between a mediocre medium and a spectacular medium is in how the medium handles a 'no' response. A brilliant medium has learnt to embrace the 'no' and to use it as a prompt to look deeper for evidence. They are skilled enough to not lose confidence and to remain in their power and trust Spirit fully. Had I not stayed in my power but given up I would have lost an important opportunity of connection and reunion for this recipient.

When receiving a number of 'no' responses, an untrained medium will immediately assume that they've got it wrong or that they can't be very good at what they do. In reality several scenarios may have occurred.

It may be that the Spirit person communicating has changed without the medium realizing. This means the information may be correct but the intended recipient has now changed. A good indication that this has happened is when you get at least three noes in a row after getting a number of yeses previously.

Another reason for a 'no' being given is that the medium might not have interpreted what they were sensing correctly. Spirit will never get it wrong. If you're getting it wrong then the solution is to master your nerves and go back to Spirit for clarification or for an alternative way to pass on the evidence. Never ask your recipient, lest you be accused of cold reading or fishing for information; Spirit is your source. This process will get easier with time and practice and will eventually become seamless for you.

Of course, in many other instances the recipient may not actually have any knowledge about a piece of evidence your Spirit person is presenting them with or, as previously stated, they may have simply forgotten. In these cases people will often respond with a 'no' rather than a more accurate 'I don't know'.

These noes, however, can become *gold nuggets* when the evidence given is later confirmed by another family member or is remembered on the way home. There's nothing more delightful and affirming than for a recipient to go home and have another verification given that's outside their immediate experience.

I sat for a client once and brought through their grandfather, who then went on to mention names of others who were standing with him in the Spirit world. I passed on the names and the relationship to the grandfather, but they could not be immediately placed. My client returned home and asked her parents, who were able to confirm the names given. She was stunned and delighted in her follow-up email to me.

Another time, early in my career, I connected with the father of my sitter, but when I mentioned him I noticed that she visibly stiffened and did not want to engage with him. Being inexperienced, I persisted with passing on pieces of information, and the woman responded each time with a very firm 'no', claiming she couldn't understand any of the information her father was telling me. Although my mediumship experience was not solid at that time, my psychic ability was very strong so I reverted to finishing her session with a psychic reading. At the end of her sitting I asked my Spirit guide why I'd got her father 100 per cent wrong and my guide informed me that her father was a compulsive liar and that I had actually got him 100 per cent right! I tactfully asked the client as I was walking her out of her session whether her father was prone to stretching the truth, and she responded rather animatedly that he was a compulsive liar, a gambler and a thief! This was a valuable lesson in trust for me and I understood that just because I was getting a 'no' it did not necessarily mean that I had in fact got it wrong.

On a final note, it's important that you do not argue with your recipient when they say 'no'. I have seen many mediums do this from the platform and it drops the energy of the room, leaving people feeling uncomfortable. More importantly, it pulls the medium out of their power and places them in their headspace, severely impacting the quality of mediumship for the rest of the event. It's far better to thank that contact for coming through, and move on to another contact.

## Developing trust

To truly open your mediumship you must develop an absolute trust in your Spirit communicator and the accuracy of the information that you're given. If there's any doubt whatsoever, the quality of your mediumship will suffer.

The trust must also extend to yourself; you must learn to back yourself. Trust is built up over time and with experience. It cannot be taught, yet once mastered it will serve you well, especially when you're deepening the evidence given and it may not make sense initially.

I recall sitting for a man who'd lost both of his brothers to the Spirit world. One of the brothers appeared to me bouncing a red cricket ball next to a dog and this image was persistent. I misinterpreted the image to mean that he must have played cricket. When I gave this statement, my client shook his head and told me that his brother hated all sports and certainly didn't play cricket. I could have lost confidence at this point but because I have full trust in the Spirit world, I said to my client that I would leave that with him to think about as it might make sense later.

Some weeks later my client returned to me and was very emotional as he shared an experience he had had the day after his reading. He took his dog for a walk along a boardwalk near the beach on a very busy day. They stopped near a fountain so that the dog could get a drink, then the dog started to pull very hard on the leash. My client looked down to see what the dog was pulling towards and there it was – the red cricket ball, waiting for him. This was a beautiful confirmation from his brother in the Spirit world that, had I not trusted in Spirit and myself, would have been dismissed. He showed me the cricket ball, which was indeed very bouncy, and has since had it encased in glass as a keepsake memory of his brother.

The man's brother in Spirit, knowing his brother was a skeptic who struggled with the idea of the afterlife, wanted to deliver evidence that was irrefutable. Suffice to say that this man is now a believer who has had immense healing as a result of this beautiful gift from the Spirit world.

## Exercises

1. Read tabloid magazines that have stories about people in them. Spirit will use these stories where appropriate as frames of reference when you're working.

2. Get out and about and meet people from all walks of life. Observe people – their features, characteristics and mannerisms.

3. Develop an interest in history and focus on key eras. Look at the fashion, the music, and historical figures. Study iconic features, stories and trends from each era so that you can pinpoint with accuracy what era a Spirit person lived in.

4. Find a partner to work with and exchange a piece of jewelry or a personal object. Tune into that item and try and bring forward evidence and information relating to the other person. Bring forward information from their early childhood, teens and adulthood.

5. Ask someone to place an item into a box without your knowledge and see if you can tune in and determine the item.

6. Practice sitting in the power and start a journal that records all insights you glean from your Spirit team.

7. Gather a few people around and organize a mini-demonstration. Practice connecting to Spirit and giving evidence to the group. Remember, they're only to answer you with a 'yes', a 'no', or 'I don't know'. Refrain from allowing them to give you any detail or ask you questions – this will pull you out of the power.

8. Similarly, practice giving one-on-one readings with a partner. Take your time and really develop the character and personality of the Spirit person. Try various ways of getting information, using all the psychic clairs.

CHAPTER 6

# Overcoming barriers to mediumship

*'The biggest obstacles in our lives are the barriers our mind creates.' ~ Jake Ducey*

There are many barriers to mediumship that have prevented mediums from walking their path. These barriers can include fear-based cultural and religious beliefs that prevent a medium from exploring their ability – but I won't be addressing those in this chapter. Rather, I will focus on common barriers to mediumship that are experienced by most developing mediums.

## Lack of trust

Arguably the biggest barrier or hurdle to exceptional mediumship is *trust*. This small word is the hardest to master when embarking on the mediumistic journey. The very tool that the gift of mediumship is translated through is also the very thing that can hinder our mediumship ability, and that tool is our *mind.*

Early in our development, but certainly not limited to just that time, the thought that we could just be making all this up may enter our mind. We might wonder if the connection we're making is a product of our overactive imagination or, at worst, a serious undiagnosed mental illness or mental breakdown.

Trust is hard to master, especially when we live in a culture and society that teaches us the very opposite of trust. We're bombarded with fear-based messages via the mainstream media, our schools, our peers and in almost every instance we're made to question ourselves. Am I good enough? Do I fit in? Am I wearing the right brand? Do I live on the right street? Will I be able to go to university? Does he/she really love me? These and thousands of other thoughts and questions are constantly swirling around in our minds like debris caught in a twister, meshing and clashing with such relentless ferocity that when we do perceive a glimmer of light in the fog we quickly question or dismiss that too. Knowing our own mind and trusting our Spirit team and ourselves is crucial.

When working as a medium, and when developing your mediumship skills, your attitude is a crucial point of distinction. If I was in the Spirit world and I wished to make a connection with my loved one, I know which medium I'd choose. It would be the one who says, 'I'm going to give this a try and I'll do my best.' I wouldn't choose the one who's thinking, 'I hope I can do this. What if I don't get anyone? Am I making this up?'. You must have total faith and belief that the Spirit world is real and that the connection you make and have is real.

How can we develop trust? The short answer: is one step at a time. The long answer is: using what I call the three Ps of mediumship – *perseverance, practice and patience*. Mediumship is not an instant unfoldment; it takes years of dedicated practice to master.

Imagine that within you is a trust bank that will be empty initially. With perseverance, practice and patience each successful positive experience will convert to trust currency that is deposited in your trust bank account. The key is to only accept deposits and not to withdraw trust if you've had an experience that hasn't gone well for you. In other words, only focus on the positive mediumship experiences and bank those.

To help with this, when commencing your initial practice I recommend you keep a *trust journal* where each success is logged. Let the non-successful moments fall away; do not dwell on them. During the times when you have a crisis of confidence in your mediumship ability, opening your trust journal will bolster your trust and reignite your power.

Isn't it interesting how quickly we forget our wins yet will dwell on a single perceived failure for months or even years to come? Change your mindset and see each perceived failure as an experiment, an opportunity for learning and subsequent refining of your ability. In this way, trust is magnified and becomes fully anchored into your psyche and the core of your being.

## Fear of being ridiculed

If you're unfortunate enough to have been born into a family that knows nothing about this gift and therefore cannot support or validate your experience, you can be left feeling very vulnerable and very alienated. It's basic human nature to want to belong in order to feel safe, to feel nurtured and to be supported. If you're not free to be yourself and to have this ability validated, you may find that soul ignition does not occur for you; rather, you might try to dim your own light in order to fit in.

Society can struggle to accept another point of view that goes against the norm. There are entrenched belief systems in society that cover religion and science and as a result there is little room to embrace the *unseen*. It takes a brave soul to stand up and speak about their beliefs in the face of fear or ridicule.

Seek out like-minded individuals, support groups or development circles where you can support each other and your development and have open and honest conversations in the Spirit of learning and sharing. When you do find one of these supportive groups you'll feel relieved and have a feeling of *coming home*. This can have a flow-on effect on your level of comfort, confidence and power.

I myself kept my ability under wraps while in a professional corporate workforce environment. Over time, as my confidence in not only my ability but who I was as a person increased, I was able to publicly own and state what I knew to be true and that was the fact that I was a medium.

It wasn't until I embraced being a medium and owned it that I noticed a shift in people's perception of me. I found that when I was struggling internally to embrace mediumship, this internal struggle and psychic shame was reflected back to me through the people I encountered. But once I spoke with confidence and power, even if people didn't agree with what I said, I was better equipped to navigate that conversation and to not be affected by it. We'll never have control over other people's opinions of us; the only thing we have control of is whether we choose to be affected by those opinions. What others think of us is none of our business. What we think of ourselves is what matters.

## Fear of failure

All mediums will face this fear at some point in their development; fear does not discriminate. It can strike at any time and in any situation and it is usually a result of an undisciplined mind.

We know that the vast majority of our fears never eventuate, yet an undisciplined mind will yield to fear, allowing fear to overwhelm and disempower it. Fear will grip a fledgling medium, paralyzing their mind, and hence will severely restrict or completely block their connection to Spirit. Fear will also grip the mind of well-known mediums that rely on reputation and public performances to increase their profile. Once you've reached a certain level of acclaim, the public expects you to always be at your peak and is not nearly as forgiving as they are towards a novice.

For some, this fear is so strong that they'll never step outside their comfort zone and try something different. In response to this dilemma I offer you this: Spirit has chosen *you* to pass on *their* messages. They've put their faith in you and they rely on you to be their voice. You can be sure that Spirit never gets it wrong – ever. With your Spirit team backing you up 100 per cent you will always succeed; mastering your own mind is essential.

In the past, I gave many readings in private sittings but didn't dare demonstrate in a public forum. The thought of all those people looking at me was quite daunting. What if I got it wrong? What if no one from the Spirit world appeared? These are common fears that affect us all. What I found was that the development of my confidence correlated to how much I practiced and stretched myself. I also found that by placing my trust in an experienced mentor, I was able to receive invaluable feedback and confirmation that gave me the confidence to move beyond my self-imposed limitations.

I am quite a shy person; however, I've developed skills to overcome this shyness and have worked hard at mastering confidence. Ironically, in most of my working career I have been thrust into public speaking or leadership roles. Clearly I was being trained for my ultimate vocation without realizing it.

When we have the right tools, knowledge and strategies in place, the fear of failure is diminished. When we stop making it about us and shift the focus to being of service to Spirit, our fear subsides. It's a mindset that must be mastered so that the quality of mediumship is not eroded.

It's natural to have some fear or nervousness. When working mediumistically, a little adrenalin will keep our minds sharp, whereas too much floods our body, overwhelming our senses and confusing our mind. A healthy balance is needed.

## Fear of hurting and not helping

All mediums work with Spirit because they have a deep desire to help and assist others. It is my belief that if we have the *intention to help* and assist then we can't get it wrong. A deep emotional intelligence and maturity is required.

When working with Spirit, there's a huge pressure on the medium to get it right, to be sure that we've interpreted the information received correctly and accurately. We need to be emotionally astute to understand if the sitter is at risk or vulnerable. This is the case for many reasons but particularly when healing or understanding is needed around abuse issues or in situations where a sitter has been impacted by suicide.

As mediums, we need to ensure that we have contact numbers at hand for mental health professionals, grief counselors and suicide prevention advocates. We cannot take on responsibility for the actions of another, but it is my belief that we do have a duty of care to pass on these details where required.

Perhaps one of the most memorable sittings I had, one which highlights this very topic, was one where a young mother came to me so that I could make contact with her husband. She had no understanding of the Spirit world and came to me with an ulterior and unspoken motive: she wanted proof that the Spirit world exists so that she could take her life and be with her beloved husband.

From the very moment I commenced her reading, her husband came through with intensity and urgency and his first words were 'Don't do it!' I immediately realized what she was planning to do and became alarmed for her.

She was a beautiful lady who was so deep in her grief that she saw no way out. My session became a combination of mediumship and counseling. Her husband went on to ask her to think of their daughter, who would be left behind, and even told her a white lie. He told her that if she took her life she would still not be reunited with him until the time that was predestined; that she would be in a virtual waiting room in the Spirit world. He did this out of love for her and to save her life.

This act of love highlighted for me that the Spirit world always act with love. I then offered to call the local hospital for her and to get her into the hands of professionals. She refused, but did take the telephone numbers with her. I asked her not to visit other mediums until at least twelve months had passed, as she was so deep into her grief and wasn't thinking clearly.

A year later, I was relieved when she returned for another sitting with me and was in a healthier state of mind than before. That sitting ended up being quite healing for her as she rejoiced in the connection with her husband. She has since gone on to study mediumship and is a wonderful ambassador to the Spirit world.

Not all sittings have happy outcomes like this one. I believe, however, that if we operate from the highest intention to help, no more can be asked of us. Sadly, there are unscrupulous mediums who, due to lack of education or training, will pass on unhelpful messages to their sitters – messages such as that their loved one in the Spirit world is in pain, trapped in limbo due to suicide, or still angry with those left behind. The Spirit world offers healing and assistance to everyone that has crossed over. Rest assured your loved ones are pain-free and at peace.

## Lack of self-love and self-worth

It is well known that a lack of self-love or self-respect causes disharmony in one's personal life. In the same way, any kind of self-worth issue we may have will cause our energy to drop, directly impacting the quality of our mediumship. For this reason, we must address these kinds of feelings as we grow in our connection to Spirit, learning to value ourselves so we may embody the highest vibration, love. After all, it is love that motivates us all to reach out and make contact.

If we don't value ourselves, this too will become a barrier to our mediumship and will hold us back. Inner dialogue such as 'Who am I to be doing this work?' speaks volumes about your level of self-worth. Many developing mediums feel like frauds, wondering if they are making up the evidence.

If you struggle with these feelings, I ask you: who are you *not* to be doing this work? There are mediums from all walks of life; some are highly educated and some are not. Your level of education and socioeconomic background do not matter to the Spirit world! What does matter is your willingness to work on behalf of the Spirit world, to assist others in their search for truth, and to demonstrate that life is eternal. It is our level of sincerity and willingness to be a channel for Spirit that establishes the quality of our mediumship. This is why Spiritual teachers throughout the ages have encouraged seekers to walk in humility, dropping the false pride that makes us overly concerned with how the world sees us.

Healing and elevating our sense of self-worth are integral to determining the type of medium we become. This healing develops as we grow in our awareness that Spirit and those who come to us for a reading are worthy of our best efforts. When we know this in our core, our insecurities fade in the face of the beauty and grace of the mediumship process. By shifting our focus to the desire to facilitate the miracle of mediumship, any sense of low self-worth lessens. We come to realize that Spirit when true surrender occurs often compensates personal weaknesses in the medium.

Remember, those who are born to serve the two worlds are also born with all the tools at hand. The only things Spirit asks you to bring are an open heart, an open mind and the desire to serve.

Knowing that love is unifying, healing and a powerful force, and witnessing love though the connections made, is a beautiful reminder that we are indeed love embodied.

# Fear of self-delusion

The fear of self-delusion is common in developing mediums. Students of Spirit often wonder, 'Am I making this up? Is it all in my head? How do I know it's really the Spirit world communicating with me?'

The fact that mediums ask these questions of themselves is a sign of healthy thinking. No one who's sincere about being an instrument of information for Spirit wants to mislead themselves or others by giving readings based upon nothing more than their imagination.

Having said this, it's important to realize that a true medium, one who undergoes training and verification of their ability, will quickly recognize their work to be authentic. Certain characteristics of Spirit will become evident. For example, a tangible shift in the energy field around the medium will be felt as the Spirit world gathers near. For some, this shift is subtle; for others, it comes with strong physical confirmation. Many times, a medium will feel a cool breeze, a fluttering in their heart or stomach, or a tingly sensation on their arms or neck. This is not a frightening experience; the energy of Spirit is loving, comforting, caring and kind. Another characteristic of Spirit is that it answers questions and provides feedback rather than providing a stream of constant chatter or a running dialogue that one is unable to switch off or control. When Spirit draws close, one is aware of a force that is intelligent, aware, and benevolent.

Once Spirit has blended with the aura of the medium, they will then go on to use the knowledge, thoughts, feelings and emotions of the medium to communicate. Even though this is occurring, the thoughts and words of Spirit will sound different to your own. The information you receive will not sound like your own thinking. The sitter is the one who will, upon receiving the information, be able to make sense of the images, words and descriptions you receive. Over time, such verification from recipients will help attune your ear to Spirit so that you can confidently distinguish between your own thoughts, ideas and feelings and the messages from Spirit.

A common fear among mediums that often remains unspoken is, 'Am I losing my mind?' I have no doubt that for some people the voices they hear are indeed a sign of mental illness, particularly if *the voices are not loving* and are urging you to harm yourself or others. As I said before, the voice of Spirit is the voice of love. This is why a development group and a proficient mediumship mentor can be so helpful. The feedback and guidance you receive will help you differentiate for yourself the true voice of Spirit. In addition, a skilled mentor will be able to read your auric field and determine where the communication is coming from. In a development group, you'll be able to speak freely about your concerns and questions without feeling pressured or judged. Rest assured, with practice and support you'll quickly learn to assimilate and integrate the method and style of communication as given by Spirit.

## Nerves

Most mediums will experience some degree of nervousness before they give a private reading or conduct a public demonstration. While it's normal and healthy to feel this way, our nerves must indeed be mastered if we're to free up our mind and heart to focus totally on the Spiritual service at hand.

How you master your nerves is an individual process that you must discover for yourself. Some people use deep breathing, meditation or relaxation techniques. Others use music or humor to overcome their nerves. The aim is not to eliminate all your nerves, but rather to not allow your state of nervousness to overcome you. As I mentioned previously, a small amount of nerves will keep your mind alert and primed while you're working.

There are many useful techniques for mastering nerves, for example mindfulness meditation, which I cover in later chapters.

A professional sporting coach will use visualizations and mindset training to instill in the athlete a belief that they are best in their field.

These techniques are repeated until the athlete believes it to be true. Similarly, to overcome their nerves, a medium must believe that every time they walk out on stage or sit at their desk, they are the best medium that ever was and that they have the full support of the Spirit world. If you can achieve this, then you have by default succeeded.

Some mediums are comfortable with their ability but the thought of standing onstage terrifies them. If this is the case for you and you truly wish to perform publicly, then take positive and active steps to overcome this. There are many courses and clubs in which you can practice public speaking to help you overcome your nerves. Consider taking an acting class or join an amateur theatre company where you can learn valuable stagecraft such as speaking with confidence, voice projection and good body posture. These activities might not be directly related to mediumship, but will facilitate a more comfortable experience on stage.

One thing you can be sure of is that once you're ignited by the power of Spirit, all nerves will drop away. If you're fully ignited, any residual nervous energy will be funneled into your mediumship as you begin to focus more on Spirit and less on the audience. As with anything, the more we do it the easier it gets. With this in mind I recommend that you continuously motivate and challenge yourself to move beyond your comfort zone.

## Fear of being possessed or taken over

The fear of being possessed may occur in novices to the world of Spirit. It comes from the many superstitions and incorrect beliefs that have been instilled into the world's cultures, religions and races over the ages. The way Spirit is usually portrayed in movies as evil, malevolent or powerful arises from a complete lack of understanding of the true nature of the Spirit world. I hope I can dispel some of the worries you might have about this subject by clarifying a few important points.

First of all, Spirit does not have the ability to possess you at any time or under any circumstance. Spirit will never take over your body or your mind or indeed any other faculty. Spirit merely blends with your own energy field or aura, like two overlapping circles. The transfer of information occurs in the overlap area.

Secondly, you do not leave your body, even when you're in deep trance; you remain in contact with your body at all times. Spirit is invited by you to blend with your aura for the purposes of communication. In other words, *you* are in control and *you* are the one who determines whether Spirit will communicate with you or not.

Naturally, just as you don't like every person you come into contact with in the land of the living, so too you might not like the feeling of certain types of Spirit people. If someone was mean or aggressive in life, you'll also sense these qualities in them in the world of Spirit. True, they might have gained insights in their new state of being that they were unable to gain while in the physical body, but as a medium you may pick up the energy they manifested while on earth. This may make you uncomfortable, but try to understand that it's not uncommon for these souls to make contact for the purposes of passing on regret or an apology to their loved ones. Bearing this in mind, the adage 'There is not *one* medium for all people but there certainly is *a* medium for all people' applies. In other words, Spirit will blend easily and make contact through a medium that resonates with them and that they feel will be able to best represent them.

Finally, remember you are in charge of opening and closing your connection. How and when Spirit works with you is entirely up to you.

## Being hypercritical

The truth is, no matter how skilled a medium becomes, there's always room for improvement, for growth is eternal! Therefore, most mediums will at times be critical of their work. In some ways, this propels them to look for ways to refine their mediumship. There's a difference, though, between critiquing your ability and a scathing attack on it. Like anything else in life, an excess of self-criticism can have the paralyzing effect of stunting or even blocking your mediumship. There are many hopeful mediums that have walked away because they haven't been able to overcome their hypercritical mind. Your soul mind will never belittle or condemn you, for it knows the efforts you're making to develop your mediumship. The egoic mind, however, is quite proficient at being hypercritical of you and often does so unchecked.

We've been raised in an environment where we're surrounded by judgment, comparisons and opinion. It takes a highly evolved person to not fall into the trap and illusion of separation. When we can move past that and know that we are all *one love* and united in this adventure called life, then the need to be critical of self or other is eliminated.

All mediums at some point will have a bad reading, a bad afternoon or even a bad day. We know that what we focus on is what expands in life, so when this occurs it's important to let these experiences go and focus only on your wins. Mediumship, although a calling, is not unlike any other profession. There's no worker in the world that could say honestly that they've never had an off day at work. Overthinking and being self-critical when a reading is less than perfect is counterproductive. It's unrealistic to expect to be 100 per cent correct 100 per cent percent of the time. Mediums are human too; like all humans they get tired, sick, and emotionally stressed.

It's when the medium is placed on a pedestal that real danger comes into play. Some mediums crumble under the unfair expectations of others. On the other hand, the medium can begin to believe their own press and fall into the illusion of superiority, becoming critical of others. Whether the result is a deflated or inflated ego, the quality of mediumship suffers. A healthy middle ground is ideal: the ability to be objective in the critique of your ability for the purposes of continuous improvement. Your trusted mentor should be able to give you an assessment of your ability and where your next opportunity for growth lies.

# Depleting your energy

Poor management of your own energy will result in poor mediumship. Being a medium means that it is your responsibility to monitor and manage your energy cycles carefully. Your energy may ebb and flow throughout the day, the week and even through the seasons and years.

You may find that over winter, for example, your energy level drops and as a result your mediumship quality diminishes. It's your responsibility to schedule your work according to your own energy biorhythms. I'd suggest that you keep a journal or diary and log your energy so that you can identify when your energy is not at peak. Knowing this allows you to schedule adequate breaks to ensure you're always at your best. Efficient use of energy comes with practice and experience and is something that's unique to each medium, their energy reserves and how they use their energy.

Mediums have an innate desire to assist as many people as possible. Quite often they go beyond their capacity and leave little room to give back to themselves. It is this desire, unchecked or out of balance, that will result in burnout and fatigue.

When giving private readings, work out how many readings you can successfully give during a day and then stick to that. Boundaries and discipline are crucial in ensuring that you don't give beyond your capacity. If you continue to deplete yourself, you'll stunt any further mediumship development. Discipline must also be used with friends and family members who may overstep boundaries by constantly asking you to read for them on demand. Give yourself permission to rest when you need to. Spirit will still be there when you return, and so will the list of people seeking assistance in connecting to Spirit.

Take time out and nurture yourself when you need to. It's not necessary to do it all yourself, or all in one day!

The level of support around a medium has a huge impact on their ability to perform their work. If you're in a home environment with many family issues going on (emotional, financial, time- or health-related), this will affect personal energy and consequently your mediumship. In such cases I recommend that you take time out to focus on and resolve the issues before resuming your mediumship practice. I promise you Spirit will still be there for you when you return; you will not lose your connection to Spirit.

Managing your energy levels during your work is critical to delivering solid readings. Eat lightly and stay hydrated so that you don't feel tired or sleepy, and use strategies to keep your energy raised – for example, during a private sitting or public demonstration make sure you don't spend too much time describing a person in Spirit, without communicating with them; this results in you using up too much of your own energy, which in turn diminishes your ability. Be self-aware and check in constantly on the quality of your energy.

## Lack of training

I'm going to preface this section by stating that I understand that all mediums are self-developed. The difference between a successful professional medium and a hobbyist medium lies in the training, commitment and dedication to Spirit.

I operated a successful practice for many years as a self-taught medium; however, it was the training I received from Mavis Pittilla that propelled me forward in my development. She clarified my experiences and gave me the language of mediumship that facilitated a deeper understanding for me.

Understanding the mechanics of mediumship gave me the ability to conduct a self-review and identify the gaps in my knowledge and development. Self-reflection was an important part of this process as I was able to contextualize my experiences and build my understanding around a solid framework of knowledge.

As a professional medium and mentor, I feel that I have a personal duty to ensure that my education is at the highest level so that what I pass on to my students is accurate and of the highest standard. To that end, I too am continuously learning and refining my mediumship. I am always a student of Spirit.

When publicly demonstrating, I understand that I'm also educating the general public as well as other developing mediums on the nature of the Spirit world and how mediumship works. Sadly, I've seen many examples of well-meaning mediums giving out incorrect information about Spirit that can give rise to, at the very least, ridicule, and at the worst, fear in the general public.

I look forward to the day when quality education and understanding of what mediumship is becomes a universal norm in society.

## Teaching too soon

Many practicing mediums will take on teaching much too soon in their own development, with detrimental results. Tempting as it is to be inspired to teach, if you are not *established and developed in your own personal power* then you can quickly deplete your energy, which will impact your own mediumship. In some cases you may even go backwards in your development or, more disastrously, lose your confidence to serve Spirit at all.

To even consider becoming a teacher or mentor, you must be putting into practice and demonstrating what you're teaching and should have a proven track record of providing exceptional guidance to others. Taking it on too soon also becomes a barrier to mediumship if you stop sitting in development circles or participating in further training. This can mean that you stagnate and stop evolving and growing. Mediumship is a constantly evolving field since humanity is continuous evolving.

Also, mediumship development takes many years of commitment and understanding, not only to acquire the skill set but to acquire insight into human nature. It is my belief that a mentor and teacher must have accumulated life experiences and wisdom in order to relate to a wider representation of the community.

In conclusion, although many potential barriers have been discussed in this chapter, it is certainly not exhaustive and no doubt you'll be able to add to the list. Ultimately, if you reduce all these barriers to the lowest common denominator you'll see that our biggest barrier is *fear*.

As you can see, fear wears many masks and disguises. A big part of your development as a medium is identifying and acknowledging what our particular fears are. It's only when we know what our personal barriers to mediumship are that we can, through discipline and practice, overcome them. Remember, it's a work in progress, and if we're truly students of mediumship it will continue for as long as we're practicing in our earthly lives. There will never be a time when we're not experimenting with new techniques and ways of deepening our connection to Spirit, so it's wise to become comfortable with the fact that there will always be more to learn.

## Exercises

1. Develop a trust journal; write in or voice record instances where trust was encountered.
2. Face and conquer one of your fears, for example by taking a public speaking course, acting classes, going bungee jumping or flying.
3. Develop a morning ritual of protection and clearing techniques that work for you.
4. Repeat a mantra such as 'I am a skilled medium and I have a brilliant connection to Spirit' for at least twenty-one days.
5. Keep an energy diary – monitor your energy over a twelve-month period and work out when you're at your peak mediumistically.
6. Work with a skilled mentor medium who's able to move you beyond your personal barriers. Seek out other kinds of mentors as well.
7. Practice mindfulness techniques and deep breathing to help you master your nerves.
8. Choose training courses that are of the highest caliber. You owe it to yourself to determine what is world-class mediumship and what is not. Only learn from those you wish to emulate and who are accomplished in their field and supportive of your development.
9. Practice saying 'no' to those who deplete your energy. Limit your time with them and filter out any negative comments. This includes family and friends.
10. Choose activities that bolster your self-worth. This may include working with a professional therapist to resolve emotional issues and fears.

CHAPTER 7

# Mediumship skills and tools

*'Good design goes to heaven; bad design goes everywhere.'*

*~ Mieke Gerritzen*

Our relationship with Spirit and how Spirit works with us is personal and a unique experience for us all. There are, however, various methods, skills and tools that are common in Spirit communication. In this chapter I will explore some of these tools and techniques that I've found useful in my practice and in my teachings.

## Grounding

Without a doubt, the first thing to learn when working energetically with Spirit is how to become grounded so that clear communication is achieved. By grounding, I mean setting up an energetic circuit between the physical Earth, your physical body and your energy body.

To understand grounding in a more tangible way, consider the antennas on the roof of our homes. These antennas receive a waveform that contains both voice and picture data that is displayed on our television sets when we switch them on.

If the antenna is not grounded properly, the image or sound we experience on our television becomes distorted. We may hear the voices but may not see the picture, or the picture we see may be fuzzy or discolored.

This is effectively what can happen to the communication we receive from Spirit. If we work while ungrounded, we may interpret the information given incorrectly or with distortion. Grounding gives us the best possible set of conditions for clear communication.

So how do we actually achieve grounding? With a little research you'll discover that there are many ways to ground, but the methods you choose will depend on what works for you.

As for me, I like to keep things simple. I've found the following technique works very well, both personally and for my students.

*Grounding technique*

1.  Sit with both feet flat on the floor beneath you.
2.  Close your eyes to center yourself and draw in a deep breath.
3.  Imagine two ruby red shafts of light emerging from the soles of your feet.
4.  Imagine those shafts of light penetrating the surface of Mother Earth and travelling down through all the layers until they reach her central magnetic core.
5.  Anchor those shafts of light into the core with intention, stating that you are now grounded.
6.  Once grounded you should be able to feel a pull downward that indicates you are now grounded.

Once mastered, this technique will become second nature for you, and you'll be able to achieve it instantaneously. In the beginning, I recommend that you do it with slow, mindful, conscious intention. Eventually, this fundamental technique – or another like it – will become a cornerstone of your practice when developing and working with Spirit. You will learn to instinctively begin your readings with this grounding, just as you will instinctively close your readings with another practice.

## Attuning the ear

When I say 'attuning the ear' I mean taking the time to learn to listen and look for Spirit all day, every day, as you go about your daily life and business, learning to decipher the language of Spirit in whatever form it's presented to you. Spirit will communicate with you in various ways, using signs, numbers, words, colors and music. Our job is to learn to discern when Spirit is actually communicating with us and when a feather, for example, is just a feather. Your Spirit team will have a particular way of communicating with you, their own signature style. As you get used to the language, tone and feeling of their communication you'll be able to identify them confidently. You'll begin to discern a shifting in the energy when Spirit draws near, feeling them essentially skim above your normal thought stream, much like a surfer surfs on the waves of the ocean.

Mastering differentiation between your own thoughts and Spirit communication takes skill, time, patience and practice. Many novices make the mistake of believing that *everything* is a sign from Spirit. Discernment is a must and knowing your own mind and how it works is crucial. It's easy to become enraptured with Spirit and to lose perspective; remaining grounded and having a critically attuned ear counteracts this, and allows you to move forward with confidence in the communication you receive from Spirit.

Over time you'll become familiar with your Spirit team and how messages are passed through you. This too will give you confidence and trust in your own abilities and in your Spirit team.

As you continue to grow and evolve you may find that members of your Spirit team change. If this occurs, try not to let it dismay you or destabilize your practice. Remember, your Spirit team is not fixed; it will change when it needs to, to ensure your continuous development and evolution as a medium and as a human being. Just as we progress through various classrooms and year levels in a school setting, so too will you encounter new teachers in your Spirit team who have deeper expertise and knowledge.

This happened to me recently when my whole Spirit team changed. Through my clairvoyance I saw my whole team pack their metaphorical suitcases and walk out of a room. This was very disconcerting and I found myself feeling like a cork floating in the ocean for a few months until I reattuned my ear to my new team. I'd become very used to how my team communicated with me and reattuning to my new team was like learning how to walk again.

Since becoming reattuned, I've adapted to the new way I receive communication and messages. If this happens to you, don't be alarmed – just take the time to determine how your new team wishes to work with you. It's important that you don't have a crisis of faith; in fact, at times like this trust is crucial. I also recommend that you consult with your mediumship tutor or mentor so that you're supported during this transition phase, while you continue to work on reestablishing your confidence and trust.

## Supporting our nervous system

Our nervous system is the tool that the physical body uses when connecting and communicating with Spirit. As we begin to work with Spirit, we need to become aware of the reactions within our nervous system. We need to become proficient in ascertaining what our nervous system is doing and understanding what this may mean.

Early on in my development when I connected to Spirit I'd start to feel my heart racing, my hands would tremble and I'd feel lightheaded and slightly nauseous. I interpreted these feeling as me getting nervous before a demonstration until over time I realized that these symptoms were simply the effects of the blend between Spirit and myself. Once I understood this connection, the intensity of the impact on my nervous system subsided.

Spirit is vibrating at a higher frequency than we are, since they don't have a heavier, dense physical body to deal with. For the blend between Spirit and the medium to be successful, Spirit has to reduce their vibration while, simultaneously, we have to increase our vibration to match frequencies as closely as possible. In this way, a clear communication link is established.

In those early days I would hear the sound created by this frequency-matching process through my clairaudience. The sound of Spirit was like a generator whining while it was being slowed down and my own frequency was like a mini-motor winding up at top speed. It was interesting that Spirit showed me this blending process by drawing upon my electronic engineering background. I was made aware of how the process works through my mental knowledge of electronics.

Knowing that our nervous system is used by Spirit to initiate communication makes us aware of how important it is to keep our system in peak condition. It is this system that is our tool of the trade and like any master craftsman who values her tools and takes meticulous care of them, so must we.

So how do we keep our nervous system in peak condition? I'm certainly not a medical professional so if you have medical concerns about your nervous system, then please see a health professional, but here are some common practices that have enhanced my own nervous system.

1. **Adequate sleep** – ensuring you get good-quality restorative sleep is a must so that you and your energy are at your best when you're working.
2. **Boundaries** – maintain strong healthy boundaries around your relationships and make sure you have the time you need

to keep you clear and aligned. These boundaries include both physical and energetic ones.

3. **Support** – having a great support network that encompasses family, friends, health care practitioners, educators, mentors and more will ensure that you and your mental health are looked after. Don't be shy about asking for and getting help when you need it.

4. **Nutrition** – finding a food choice style that suits your body and its needs is crucial to keeping your energy at its peak. Don't be swayed by health fads or what works for others around you. Your body knows best what it requires, so make sure that you listen to it.

5. **Stress minimization** – keeping your stress levels as low as possible will ensure your body performs at its best. This is often a moving goal post as you navigate life and all the milestones that come with it, including family, marriage, divorce, children, bereavement, and more.

6. **Rest** – take the time to rest and retreat when you need to. You don't have to be available to people and their needs all the time. It isn't selfish to put your needs above those of others; it's part of taking care of yourself so you can have the strength needed to serve your loved ones well. This includes taking a break from your mediumship should you need to restore and recharge your energy.

## Sitting in the power

This is a fundamental tool of mediumship and possibly the most useful in your tool kit. Many of you may already be doing this naturally without realizing it; however, without intention and focus you may not be maximizing the results.

What do I mean when I say 'sitting in the power'? Quite simply, we're readying ourselves generally and our energy specifically to become receptive to the Spirit world. It's not a meditation process, as some mistakenly believe. In meditation, we're sitting *passively* and relaxing our energy bodies. In contrast, sitting in the power *charges* our energy field.

Sitting in the power need not be a complicated process but it's essential that you sit at a time when you're not likely to be disturbed. I also recommend that you sit in silence, without any distracting background music, so that you can be truly at one with that spark of divinity that resides within your own soul. Exercise 2 at the end of this chapter describes how to sit in the power.

Make an intention that you are going to sit in the power and then feel your power growing and becoming charged within you. Each medium will experience this in ways that are unique to them. Some of the signs of the power building within you are feeling a pulsing in your solar plexus, increased heat, trembling, or a quickening of energy in your heart center, to name but a few. I love a description that my mentor Mavis gave in a lecture on sitting in the power: she likened it to the feeling of bubbles rising up inside a champagne bottle. I'll add to this that the more practiced you become the finer the bubbles become. There's a marked difference between savoring a fine vintage bottle of champagne versus a cheaper one; time and effort are key ingredients to achieving quality.

It's recommended that you sit in the power at least once a week, but preferably two or three times a week. Once you're in sitting in the power with some regularity you may also wish to sit with your main guide and Spirit team, in order to develop a good, strong relationship with them. The difference here is that you're setting an intention to have a conversation with your main guide, versus sitting in the power to build your energetic muscle.

Dedicate an assigned time each week to do this, then make sure you keep your appointment time. Not only is this good discipline, it's also good manners; respect the time that your Spirit team have set side to dedicate themselves to you.

Once again, be aware that this time is *an opportunity for dialogue*, not for you to sit passively, waiting for a download of information, teachings or wisdom. You're there to interact, to share and learn from each other. Sitting in passive receptivity will not bring you the results you want – this would be like turning up to a meeting and then simply staring at the attendees, hoping they'll somehow know what it is you wish to discuss.

In the beginning you might find that very little conversation flows. Don't be discouraged! Spiritual dialogue is an art, just as it is in human relationships. Be open to building your dialogue and conversation over time as you learn to attune yourself to your team, and vice versa. Remember, this is a two-way street, and your contacts are also learning how best to communicate with you.

It's imperative that you build a level of trust between you and your main guide. This can be a lifetime friendship that, if you take the time to foster it, will serve you well in your mediumistic and personal development into the future. Believe me, you'll never feel alone again once this link is established.

## Raising your vibration

Any activity, ritual or exercise that you do that makes you feel lighter and happier is an excellent way to increase your frequency, thus making communication with Spirit easier. The clearer you are, the higher your vibration becomes.

Spirit loves laughter, and laughter is a fun and instant means of raising the vibration of the energy around you. Through enjoying comedy or having a robust sense of humor you're naturally aligning yourself to Spirit communication.

Another way of raising your vibration is to play uplifting music. Compile a playlist of songs that instantly give you a lift. Music has an instant effect on our psyche and on our mood; any genre can be used, as long as it has an impact on you personally.

Energy-building activities such as qi gong, tai chi or yoga, although not absolutely necessary to achieve communication, go a long way towards keeping your energy high. Taking time out to rest and recharge is also a good idea; the more we look after ourselves, the less taxing Spirit communication becomes on our physical bodies.

As my development has progressed over the years and my connection has deepened, I found that my choices in life have also changed. I found that I progressively eliminated or greatly reduced alcohol, sugar and dense foods from my life. I now choose organic and live whole food where possible. My water intake is alkaline and all products I use on my person and in my home are natural and organic-based. This has been a gradual transition in my life; I didn't sit down one day and decide to make radical changes. I just found that it became a way of life for me.

This change was also reflective of family and friendship groups, where my relationship with toxic people has been restricted or eliminated. If an encounter with someone leaves you feeling drained or depleted, ensure you take adequate steps to minimize contact. If you wish to remain in contact, find ways to enter such an environment without being negatively affected.

Once again, getting good-quality sleep goes a long way towards keeping your vibration at a high level. If your sleep quality isn't good, then communication becomes foggy and unclear. If your mental mind is not at peak performance, your quality of work will reflect this. I realize, of course, that life has its ups and downs and losing sleep is bound to occur at times. I've found that at times like these, short naps or a period of meditation can help restore a feeling of refreshment. In some cases you may wish to reschedule your appointments to a time when you're feeling better. Personal integrity and being responsible for your work is of paramount importance.

## The mind journey

The *mind journey* is a delightful tool to use when communicating with Spirit. If you can faithfully set aside the time needed to experience this, you may achieve spectacular results!

So what is a mind journey? It's a method of joining with the mind of Spirit and asking questions, much as an investigative journalist might do. If during a reading Spirit shows us, for example, a fob watch, we have the option of simply passing on this singular piece of information to the recipient, or we can deepen the evidence by taking the mind journey. We can ask Spirit why this watch was shown, where it is currently, who wore it, where it's from, when it was acquired, and why. Allow your natural curiosity to take the lead and follow a deeper line of questioning. This can produce some excellent confirmation for the sitter, as sometimes the best verification is found in the details. Don't be afraid to mention the small, seemingly insignificant observations you make. They may sound odd at first, but most likely will have special meaning to the sitter.

Another way of going on the mind journey is by asking Spirit to mentally walk you through the home of the sitter or their Spirit person. Utilizing your clairvoyance, look around your environment and observe the details: décor, the pictures on the walls, color schemes, furniture, windows and scenery and so forth. Describe what you see to your sitter as it appears to you. This fascinating type of mind journey experience feels as if you're looking through Spirit's eyes.

I recall a demonstration where I brought through a woman's father from the Spirit world, that took me first to his former place of work. I could clearly see that he was involved in outdoor construction. He then showed me how he used to sketch designs on scrap paper during his break. I asked questions about the sketches and he showed them to me – they were structures such as bridges and buildings. Probing deeper, I asked him if he was an engineer or draftsman and he showed me his handmade drafting table, located in his home office. When I passed all this information on to his daughter she was delighted with the amount of detailed evidence because it confirmed for her without a doubt that this was her father, who was indeed a draftsman.

If I'd passed along only the fact that he worked outside, I would have missed the crucial evidence of the homemade drafting board that was unique to this man. As you can see, remaining inquisitive and employing the tool of a mind journey, even for a few moments, is immensely useful in conveying the deeper essence of the person in Spirit, for it moves us beyond basic physical descriptions, which, while useful, don't always convey the uniqueness of the person in the Spirit world.

## Symbology

Spirit will utilize any means possible to communicate with us, be it literal or more commonly through the use of symbology. All stored memories, experiences and knowledge a medium has accumulated over their lifetime may be accessed by Spirit and then used to convey a message.

This stored information may be brought back to the conscious mind as a literal reference or as a symbolic reference. The challenge for the developing medium is to determine if the information given is symbolic or literal. The ability to do this is built up over time, with experience.

The medium has to build a library of symbols and reach an agreement with their Spirit team as to the meaning of each symbol for them. *This library of symbology will be unique to each medium and their own Spirit team.*

For example, when I see the earth as a globe, I know from experience and the agreements I've made with Spirit that they're referring to someone who's still on the earth plane. If reference to a specific date is given and I'm also shown a cupcake, then I know that Spirit is referring to a birthday.

There are no hard and fast rules about symbology other than making sure you and your Spirit team are aware of, and adhere to, the agreed meanings. Over time and with continued practice and experience your library of symbols will grow so that you can very quickly determine what Spirit is communicating.

I cover signs and symbology in more depth in the next chapter, but am flagging it here since it's a major tool of the trade.

## Mirroring

This technique is used by Spirit to highlight where certain conditions existed in the Spirit person's former physical body. For example, if they had a sore right hip during their life, the medium may also feel pain in the hip and be able to pass on this evidence accurately. A developing medium must be careful to determine whether they've received information directly mirrored (in the exact location the Spirit person had pain) or transposed (feeling it in the opposite side of the body.) With this understanding you'll be able to accurately communicate it to your sitter. Over time and with confirmation from your sitters you'll be able to identify what kinds of ailments the Spirit person had, as well as the manner in which they passed.

Of course, this list of tools and skills is not exhaustive and no doubt as the Spirit world continues to evolve, so too will the methodology of contact. Stay open to continuous learning and let the Spirit world lead the way, always prepared to experiment and to pioneer new ways of communication.

**Exercises**

1. Practicing grounding – imagine that you're dropping anchors from both feet into the ground and be aware of how you're feeling. Now raise those anchors and notice what effect this has. Once again, drop the anchors and observe the difference in feeling. Compare and contrast these sensations several times. This will help you become attuned and present to your body and your energy field, particularly when you find yourself feeling ungrounded.

2. Practice getting into the power. Ground yourself and imagine drawing up Mother Earth's energy through your feet. Bring your focus to your base chakra, situated at the tip of your tailbone. Imagine and feel your energy start to spiral, like a vortex, out from the base chakra and feel it lifting and continuing to spiral through each successive chakra as they become energized. Stop at the third eye if your intention is to communicate only with passed loved ones from the world of Spirit. Only proceed to the crown chakra if you wish to contact more evolved people and beings from the world of Spirit, such as ascended masters or Inspirers.

3. Get into the habit of communicating with your Spirit team just as you wake from your sleep in the morning. This is when your mind is most clear and therefore communication will be easier. By beginning your day this way, you'll set the tone for the rest of your day.

4. When you're walking in nature, take the time to tune out your inner mind chatter and tune into the life force evident in nature. Notice the texture and shape of the leaves, the sounds of the birds and wildlife and the colors of your environment. This walking meditation will shift your energy field, allowing you to blend seamlessly with Spirit.

5. Practice the mind journey by sitting for a friend's loved ones who you did not know and describing a room in their house. Take your time and really explore, focusing in on details such as photo frames on sideboards, types of furniture and where they were placed.

6. Read or study an anatomy and physiology book to become familiar with the biology of the body and potential diseases it is affected by.

7. Build a symbol library covering generally accepted symbol meanings, together with the ones that are unique to you.

8. Take a class or perform activities that raise your vibration, such as yoga, tai chi, martial arts, qi gong or dancing.

CHAPTER 8

# Signs

*'Language, in its origin and essence, is simply a system of signs or symbols that denote real occurrences or their echo in the human soul.' ~ Carl Jung*

There is an old adage that says, 'Ask and you shall receive.' I believe this applies to Spirit and the signs we receive from them to answer our questions, or to let us know that they're around.

I have an agreement with Spirit that if they wish me to take note, they need to give me signs in threes. 'Why threes?' you may ask. Who knows! It's been like this for me since I became aware of this phenomenon. When I see something repeating three times I know Spirit is asking me to notice, to sit up and take heed.

Spirit walks with us and among us, endeavoring to bring to our attention signs that they are with us. The signs Spirit gives us come in many forms – subtle and obvious, humorous and serious, familiar and unusual – but once we become aware and receptive to them, we quickly realize that Spirit is in constant communication with us.

Years ago, when I first moved to Melbourne, I found myself feeling assaulted by the frenetic movement of this large city. Traffic moving at frenzied speeds, a cocktail of lights and sounds, unfamiliar roads and neighborhoods, all challenged my mental equilibrium. Driving in Melbourne I had to negotiate multi-lane freeways, overpasses, on ramps and exit ramps, not to mention the notorious hook turns in the city.

I recall one evening I took a wrong turn in the city and ended up in a place that was completely unfamiliar to me. As I was travelling along a particular road I became overwhelmed and fearful of being lost at such a late hour. The road looked the same to me in both directions and I had no idea if I was travelling towards or away from the city. Not being a native of Melbourne, I was unable to orient myself since there were no familiar landmarks, and this was before GPS systems were invented.

As a sensitive, it's easy for me to become highly stressed and with no way to navigate my way home I became quite fearful that I would not be able to find my way. In despair, I called out aloud to my guides, 'I just need a sign! Please give me a sign!' In this moment of surrender, I immediately felt calmer and my mind became clear. I drove a little farther, and something made me turn off the road I was lost on. As I made the turn, there in front of me was a sign – literally! My suburb was listed on the traffic sign and I was able to return home in ten minutes.

This was a valuable lesson for me, for I became aware that Spirit would always help as long as you remember to ask. Asking is important, for we always have free will and Spirit will not normally step in unless we give them permission to do so.

As my relationship with Spirit has strengthened over time I've become aware of various signs that they use to communicate with us. I've compiled the following list to illustrate what I've learnt. As always, this list is certainly not exhaustive but it does represent categories of signs given.

# Repetition

Any type of repetition is Spirit's way of grabbing our attention. I know I'm not alone when I see repetitive patterns of numbers such as 11-11, 222, 444 or 333, to name but a few. It's my belief that the ability to recognize patterns in our world is a survival mechanism for humans. Therefore, this ability is hardwired and instinctual for us; we're designed to take notice of patterns. Our natural world is also filled with patterns and because these patterns are universal, they transcend language barriers. This is why music and the familiar shapes found in nature resonate at such a deep level within people, no matter what culture or country they are from.

Spirit will always strive to communicate with us using methods and techniques that are latent or pre-existing in our soul. Drawing upon our inherent pattern recognition allows us to assign significance to number repetition, word repetition or seeing the same item, experience or outcome repeated.

Many people who are on the ascension path will report that they continue to see repeating numbers, especially the 11-11 sequence. I know when I'm going through internal changes the 11-11 phenomenon is prevalent in my life; for me, it represents a period of change and elevation. I began to see 11-11 on car number plates, on timepieces, on people's tattoos and other places very early in my development and I took this sign to be a wake-up call for me.

I'm not going to define what all the number sequences mean as there are hundreds of books and articles online that cover their meanings. I will, however, encourage you to conduct your own research and work out what the numbers, colors or other symbols mean for *you* and *your Spirit team*. Agree on a convention and stick to that when you're working with Spirit.

# Music/songs

Music is universal to the collective consciousness of the human race; we respond and react to it irrespective of what race or culture we belong to. For this reason, it's used often by Spirit to bridge the two worlds. Have you ever found that no matter what radio station you've turned to, the same song is playing? This is definitely a sign from Spirit. I urge you to take note of the song's lyrics or message.

I have a beautiful guide in the world of Spirit whom I refer to as my *DJ guide*. This guide will bring messages to my attention through the use of music and, in particular, songs. There are many instances where I'll hear in my mind through clairaudience words and music to a particular song that will later prove to be significant. When I notice or concentrate on the words, I find that the words I'm drawn to will give me a direct answer or clue to an issue I had been mulling over.

Another way songs can be used by Spirit is to pinpoint a particular era or decade. The generational connection to a song can be very useful when you're demonstrating or giving readings. Take your time to identify key songs that are representative of a certain time in history and observe how they become part of your bank of symbols. Learn what they are so that you can zero in on an era very quickly when you're working with Spirit.

The songs referenced may include songs that were played at a funeral, a wedding song, the favorite song of the Spirit person, or a playlist that has special meaning. In my mediumship practice, I receive a lot of evidential information via music that goes deeper than the song title – for example, there are instances where the song artist has the same name as the person in Spirit. As a medium, our job is to determine which of these scenarios applies and this can best be achieved by asking your Spirit communicator directly.

## Billboards

Oftentimes, Spirit will bring to our attention to words or messages written on billboards that we might not normally notice. I've had many occasions where I've driven past the same billboard daily, never noticing the images, let alone the words. Yet that same billboard will come sharply into focus, providing an answer I can relate to, once I've asked for a sign.

I have a beautiful friend who works in the city and often catches trams to get around; she loves to read billboards on buses and trams and swears by this means of divination. She's noticed that whenever she requires guidance a tram will go by at the right time with a billboard that gives her an answer.

When conducting readings Spirit will often flash a billboard up in my mind's eye with evidence that is pertinent for the sitter. It may be the name of a musical that is relevant, or the name of a place of employment, or even tag lines such as Nike's 'Just do it'. These are cues given by Spirit for our own enlightenment, or so that we can accurately convey their messages to those who need them. I'd recommend that you study billboards so that you have them in your memory banks as a reference for Spirit to draw upon. This includes any company logos and tag lines that are brought to your attention and awareness.

## Numbers

Repeating numbers is by far one of the most universally accepted means of receiving signs. As previously stated, the most common number combination is 11-11, which various Spiritual teachers attribute specific meanings to.

While there are universal number interpretations, there are also numbers that are unique and special for each person. My advice is to determine what certain numbers mean specifically to you. Your Spirit team will always use numbers that mean something special to you, such as a birthday, anniversary date, or a year of passing. Be open to receiving signs in this way.

Numerical signs often appear on car number plates and on clock faces, or spoken as a number combination on the radio. Have you had the experience of looking at a clock over and over at precisely the same time on different days? Notice your thoughts and feelings at that time as clues to what the numbers could mean.

There are also many books that cover angel numbers, universal numbers and, of course, numerology in general. Spirit will use what you already know, and if you're a numbers person they'll make a point of using numbers to convey messages for you.

## Butterflies, dragonflies, feathers, rainbows and birds

These universal symbols are also used by Spirit to let us know that they're around. Many people have reported that while they were thinking of their loved ones, a butterfly, dragonfly, or other element of Nature suddenly appeared, often out of nowhere.

I have a dear friend whose father had transitioned to the Spirit world. In the days leading up to his funeral, she was standing in the garden near his favorite tree and asked him to show her a sign that he was around. Immediately, a bird landed on the tree and looked directly at her, chirping animatedly. Because her father was an avid bird lover, she recognized this to be a sign of his presence.

Another very common sign from Spirit are feathers. On a personal level, feathers are definitely a confirmation that my guides are around. One year while I was still working in the corporate world, undergoing a rapid opening of my Spiritual abilities, I received an incredible sign from Spirit through feathers. I entered my office one morning to find that pure white bird feathers completely covered my desktop and office floor! To fully appreciate this, you must know that my office was on the second floor of a brand new building that did not have external windows. I locked it nightly and no one else had access to it, yet when I arrived all those feathers were waiting for me. Even maintenance was at a loss as to how the feathers got in there!

As mentioned before, the key to interpreting signs is recognizing when one is an actual sign rather than an unrelated coincidence. In my experience, if it's a sign you get an internal urging to stop and take notice of the item or event, a sense of its importance. For example, one day while rushing out the front door I noticed a feather sitting on top of a piece of paper at the foot of a statuette that sat to one side of the front door. Even though I was in a hurry, I felt a strong urge to backtrack and pick up the paper. I turned it over and there was one word written on it: 'mine'. I'd been thinking about buying the house I was in and this was a strong confirmation for me that it would happen. I realized that the feather was there to attract my attention to the piece of paper.

## People

Signs also come through certain people along the path of life. For example, you may be dealing with a question or dilemma and ask Spirit to send you a sign for guidance. Soon after, in a very synchronistic way, someone may approach you, seemingly out of the blue, to give you an answer to your question. When this occurs, it's certainly not a random event; Spirit is supplying your need.

This happened to me when my daughter as a newborn was constantly screaming in pain when she turned her head to one side but not the other. I took her to the pediatrician, who informed me that although her range of neck motion was restricted on one side, it was nothing to worry about and she would grow out of it. I was not comfortable with this answer and asked for a sign to be given to me as to what to do next. The following day while out at lunch I overheard a woman at the table next to me talking about a pediatric chiropractor who had changed her daughter's life. I excused myself for eavesdropping and asked for further details.

Later that afternoon I was with the maternal health nurse when I looked up at the noticeboard and saw an advert for a pediatric chiropractor. Then, a couple of days later, I turned on the radio and heard an advert for the same chiropractor. There were my three signs and of course I booked my daughter in without delay. That night, I had a completely changed child. No screaming, and she slept soundly for twelve hours!

# Dreams

Many people receive messages and signs from Spirit in the dream state. Dreams may be prophetic or predictive about the future; a reunion, where your passed loved one is speaking with you; or instructional, where you receive answers to questions you might have.

Spirit will use your dream state because this is the time that your mental or conscious mind is asleep, or at the very least quiet. Spirit is able to avoid the constant noise and chatter and give us messages we can understand and retain. I find my dreams are most meaningful around the 5 am – 7 am time period – the time we've completed our last deep sleep cycle and are starting to awaken into our lighter sleep.

It can be a useful practice to ask your Spirit guides a question and request that you receive an answer in your sleep state. Have a journal on hand near your bedside table so that you can jot down any insights you gain in your dreams.

# Physical phenomena

Spirit also gives us physical signs that they're around, and the methods they use are widely varied. I've witnessed coins from the year of someone's birth or death materializing, for example. Many people have reported that lights will flicker when they've been thinking about their loved ones or that they smell scents that were significant to them. This can include anything from perfume to cigars to freshly mown grass, depending on what the Spirit person was connected to in life. Others have reported how electronics may spontaneously come on or playlists may change to a song associated with a loved one. My own maternal grandfather lets me know he's around by flicking my kettle on and off, even at times when it isn't plugged in!

*A word of caution – don't assume all unusual electrical activity is from Spirit! If you notice anything askew, get your wiring and appliances checked by a qualified electrician to eliminate the risk that the appliance or wiring is faulty.*

I have a friend in the US who teamed up with another person to ask for a sign she wished to see. Her mother had a terminal illness, and she was caring for her at home and could rarely leave the house, so they decided that a sign would manifest for her but appear to the other person, who was more likely to encounter it as she was more out and about. They chose the symbol of a horse, and asked that it appear in a very unusual and unmistakable way. Within a few days, the friend attended a 4th of July barbeque at a suburban home in an area definitely not zoned for horses. There was a loud band playing at the party and someone called in a complaint to the City. As she stood on the porch, six large, beautiful horses walked into the yard with policemen on their backs! They were patrolling the neighborhood, keeping an eye on the parties going on at the beach, and had received the call to check out the noise level. One of the horses walked across the yard to the porch and nudged the shocked woman with its nose, increasing the impact of the sign. Needless to say, my friend was thrilled to hear that her friend had been given the sign she'd hoped for in a most dramatic way.

Many times, signs will come through the written word. You may be drawn to a bookshelf only to have a book fall at your feet with just the information you need. This happened to me early in my awakening when I visited a local bookshop to buy a novel to read. While perusing the titles I was literally knocked on the head by a book that fell off the top shelf. It was a book about Spirituality and awakening your psychic ability. Talk about trying to get my attention!

At other times, doorbells may ring, but when you answer nobody's there. There may be tappings and rappings on walls, or items may be moved even though you know with certainty no one in the household has moved them.

Someone I know was awakened by a loud pounding on the walls of her house one night. She searched for the source of the noise and couldn't find it, so returned to bed. Later on, she was awakened by the feel of someone grabbing her foot. She sat up and saw her former mother-in-law standing at the foot of her bed, illuminated by the early morning light. She knew her mother-in-law was currently in the hospital, recovering well from surgery, and couldn't understand how she'd gotten across town and into her house at 6 am. Her mother-in-law appeared distressed and said, 'Get my son to the hospital,' then promptly vanished. The woman immediately got up, realizing that her mother-in-law must have appeared in Spirit, and called her ex-husband. He was indeed having a medical emergency and she assisted him in contacting his brother to take him to the hospital. It was then she found out that her former mother-in-law had died shortly before she'd banged on the walls of the house and appeared at the foot of her bed.

These are all wonderful examples that Spirit is near, comforting and communicating with you through signs. Remember, these signs are there to encourage, comfort and guide you, not to frighten or confuse you. If you have any questions about how Spirit is sending you signs, have a dialogue with your guides or your passed loved ones and work out with them how you'd like to receive your signs and communication. Spirit will always honor our requests and accommodate what we're most comfortable with. People who are highly superstitious or have fear-based thinking are at risk of misinterpreting signs as *bad omens*, or even hauntings. Trust and know that signs are always given with love and strive to receive them in the same way.

On a final note: when working with signs, allow them to present themselves; there is no need to look too hard for them. Spirit will always give us signs gently and with love. The real art to understanding signs is to see the beauty or gift in them, no matter how small or subtle they might be.

**Exercises**

1.  Keep a signs and dream journal, noting down the signs you receive and how they relate to you.
2.  Research what the numbers mean and how they apply to you. There are many publications and a lot of information on the internet that will help you with this. Consider studying numerology through classes or workshops.
3.  Experiment with asking to be shown an answer to a question and then staying open to receiving the communication.
4.  With a like-minded friend, agree upon a sign you'd like to receive from your teams to signify their presence in your lives. Together, visualize the sign you wish to see and then release the expectation freely. It's fabulous to have a partner to share the excitement with when that sign comes along!
5.  Study logos, billboards and tag lines to increase your mind's references for Spirit to use.

CHAPTER 9

# Giving readings

*'Where we love is home. Home that our feet may leave, but not our hearts.'*

*~ Sir Oliver Wendell Holmes*

In order to discuss the methodology of giving a mediumship reading, be it in a private setting or as a public demonstration, we must first examine why it is that a person will seek out the services of a medium. It is my belief that they consult with a medium to get comfort and closure after the loss of their loved ones. Of course there are some who are merely curious about the afterlife. Others are skeptical and wish to find out for themselves if communication with the Spirit world is indeed possible.

Irrespective of the nature or circumstances of passing, at the very least your sitter wishes to find out the following information during their reading:

- Has my loved one survived death?
- Is my loved one OK now?
- Who are they with in the Spirit world?

These questions form the basis of any reading, while the rest of the reading is filled with evidential information that verifies that you have the Spirit person in question present, plus any messages they wish to pass on.

## How soon is too soon after a loss?

The sitter will often come to us in a state of grief and it is imperative that we conduct a reading when their grief is not acutely raw. The sitter may not be in the right mental state to receive evidence and confirmation from the Spirit world and their actions based on the reading can be unpredictable or cause them further harm. A medium has a responsibility to never pass on information that will cause harm to the sitter.

From the medium's' perspective, being highly empathic, it can be painful and traumatic to feel such grief and then try to stay in the power while communicating with the passed loved one. This can be overcome with experience and through being disciplined in your mind and energy management. You're of little use to your sitter if you're crying your eyes out.

There's no hard and fast rule as to how soon to come for a reading; however, I do recommend advising your client that at least twelve months from the time of passing is the earliest you can sit for them. This will give them time to process their grief and to become ready to hear from the Spirit world. Of course, Spirit is instantly accessible from the moment they pass into the Spirit world, and some sitters are able to cope with an earlier reading.

## Allegiance and integrity

When giving readings it's important to recognize that first and foremost our allegiance is with Spirit. That is not to say that our sitter is not important – of course they are. We are, however, employed in service to Spirit. For me the person in the Spirit world is my most honored and sacred guest. I'm inviting them into my office to chat and, as such, I always treat them with the utmost respect. If they've taken the time to communicate with and through me, I will endeavor to do my absolute best to ensure their messages are passed on responsibly, with respect and discernment.

The second thing I wish to discuss is honesty and integrity in mediumship readings; if we're utilizing our psychic senses and Spirit is not present, then we need to communicate this honestly to our sitter. There's nothing wrong with giving psychic readings; there is, however, everything wrong with passing off psychic readings as mediumship. It's critical, therefore, that we are experienced and knowledgeable enough to know the difference; to recognize when Spirit is present and when Spirit is not. The general public already uses the terms 'psychic' and 'medium' incorrectly and interchangeably, and as professional mediums it is our responsibility to educate the public.

I think it's important to point out here that when a client requests a reading, it is natural for them to have in mind something they hope to hear or someone they wish to communicate with. Do advise them, though, not to let their hopes block them from experiencing whatever and whomever comes through. It's best not to have certain requirements considered as definitive *proof* of contact with Spirit, for there may be other loved ones or messages that Spirit deems more important to bring to them. Encourage your clients to come to the reading with an open mind and heart.

## Staying open to all the clairs

During a reading Spirit will always give multi-sensory information; in other words, they will offer their message through any and all of the five psychic senses. Each medium will gravitate towards the psychic clairs in which they're strongest and most comfortable. Ideally, however, a skilled and practiced medium will look for information using all the psychic senses in order to deepen the evidence given, rather than simply relying on their dominant psychic sense or senses.

For example, if Spirit showed you a black wallet you could simply say, 'I'm being made aware of a wallet'. When expanding your senses you can add other information, for example: 'I'm being made aware of a black wallet, I can smell the leather and I know that coins were carried in this wallet because it's very heavy. I also know that this person did not like spending money, because they tell me this.'

From this example you can see how expanding your awareness to utilize all your psychic senses further enriches and deepens the evidence you're giving and gives insight into the character of your Spirit person. This approach allows the sitter to feel emotionally connected to the Spirit person and by default feel comforted that they are present and indeed enduring. The reading becomes an intimate and healing experience for your sitter as you bring their loved one to life.

## Creating the right environment

It's far easier to give a reading when the environment you're conducting the reading in is suitable. By far the biggest hindrance to giving a reading is noise. Ensure where possible that the environment you're in is not noisy. A noisy environment will distract you, causing you to utilize and expend far more energy than normal to maintain your power. Having a quiet environment will also ensure a clear voice recording if you're going to record your readings.

Make sure your environment is inviting, clean and presents well. Create an atmosphere of peace and serenity. Ensure the room temperature is just right: too hot and your energy will be sapped; too cold and it will be uncomfortable. Ensure that you and your recipient feel comfortable and safe at all times. A distracted recipient will impact on your ability to stay in the power.

During a reading people may become upset or teary once contact is made with Spirit; ensure that tissues and a glass of water are available. Maintain sensitivity and awareness around whether it's appropriate for you to continue or not, based on your client's reactions. Be mindful of your sitter's mental state. It's ok to ask a distressed client if they wish to continue to receive information in your reading.

If you're working from home, make sure that you have a zoned, dedicated space that is clean, with minimal personal items on display. Ideally, it should be separated by a physical barrier such as doors, or have an external access. Maintaining good boundaries and separation between the private you and the professional you will serve you well as it allows you to switch off when you're not working.

Creating the right environment also applies if you're reading over the internet on applications such as Skype or Zoom. Make sure your lighting is bright and people can see you. Be well presented and look behind you to check what's visible on your screen, ensuring that the space is tidy, your laundry isn't showing, and people aren't walking behind you.

## Opening your mediumship for a reading

Preparing yourself to give a reading is essentially a three-step process. The three steps outlined below ensure you're primed and ready to make contact with the world of Spirit. Be confident that Spirit is around you at all times. They are merely on an alternative frequency band, much like analogue radio is on another band to digital radio.

### Step 1

Get into the power by imagining that you're dropping an anchor from your feet into Mother Earth, establishing an earth connection for grounding purposes. Next, focus on your base chakra and, holding the intention that you're raising your vibration and energy, spiral your energy like a vortex through each chakra. If your intention is to read for people who have lost family members, then only open up to the third eye chakra, and not beyond to the crown chakra. Opening the crown will allow you to move beyond passed loved ones and communicate with higher-level beings from within the Spirit world.

**Step 2**

Command your logical mind to leave the room so that you can become a clear and pure mediumistic communication channel.

**Step 3**

Ask Spirit to blend with you and then give your reading to your recipient. As you progress in your development you'll develop your own rituals and intentions around connecting and communicating with Spirit. My advice is to keep it simple.

A purely mediumistic reading will take approximately thirty to forty-five minutes to complete, depending on the number of Spirit contacts present. If you're keeping your appointments to an hour then you may also need to incorporate some psychic information as well. There's nothing wrong with this approach as long as you're not trying to pass off a psychic reading as a mediumship reading. Complete honesty and integrity are essential to the foundation of your mediumship.

It's important to maintain focus and discipline at all times during your reading. In a private sitting where you have the luxury of time it's useful to build up information that confirms the Spirit person and then to share the memories that touch both the sitter and Spirit. Your sitter above all wishes to feel reunited with their loved ones and the most effective way we do this is through the sharing of precious memories, the stories that defined the lives of their loved ones.

## Structure of contact

Traditionally, the structure employed by Spiritualist mediums is the CERT process, which is defined as follows:

**C** **Communicator** – make a link to the Spirit world and establish who the communicator is.

**E** **Evidence** – give evidence that irrefutably demonstrates a link to that specific Spirit person.

**R** **Reason** – give the reason why that Spirit person has appeared.

**T** **Tie it up** – recap who the communicator was and the evidence and message given before moving to the next contact.

Spiritualist mediums are required to follow the CERT process in exactly this order for all contacts made when taking the platform in a Spiritualist church environment. This structure is certainly useful when you're first starting out, to keep you focused and on track, but I'd advise not adhering to this formula too rigidly. Losing rigidity in the process will allow space for unexpected yet delightful opportunities for Spirit to flavor the demonstration with their unique personality traits. These spontaneous moments that Spirit periodically gifts us with during a reading or demonstration become 'Wow!' moments for the sitter.

If Spirit wants to tell their story first, for example, yet you're trying to funnel them into revealing who they are, you'll hinder the flow of power and not get the same emotional connection to that person. Can you imagine how frustrating it would be for you if you have a really exciting story to tell and the person you're telling it to starts questioning you first, asking your name, how old you are, how tall you are and what your relationship to them is? This is what it's like for your Spirit person. They're actual people with personalities, feelings and emotions. They deserve to be treated with respect and with genuine interest in what they have to say. Have a conversation with them rather than using a checklist of questions.

Our mediumship should never be prescriptive because life is not prescriptive; our lives are rich and colorful and each life has huge variations. If we stuck to uniformity in our reading style we'd become bland clones of each other and not very interesting to listen to. Don't be afraid to explore your own unique style and way of working with Spirit. Be flexible and open-minded. Find a style or process that works for you and bring your own personality and style into your work.

Building on the CERT process, an example of a basic structure to use – in no particular order – can be as follows:

1. Who are you? Is it family, a friend, work colleague, someone from mother's side or someone from father's side? Get a name if possible, (only when your power peaks), although this is not always necessary.

2. In a public demonstration, go directly to an audience member where possible or at the very least to an area of the audience you *know* that you're being drawn to.

3. Look for the evidence. What were the last words spoken, how did they pass, where did they pass, who was with them. Your Spirit contact should be confirmed within three to four statements before messages are passed on.

4. Look at the reason the person has come. Why are they here? Is it to say hello, to offer words of support or encouragement to their family, or to pass on information about what's happening in the recipient's life right now.

5. Reassure the recipient that they're not alone by sharing a story about them and pass on any specific messages.

6. Pass on thanks from the Spirit contact to the recipient.

7. After the sitting or demonstration and at the end of your working day, sit with your Spirit contacts and ask them for an appraisal. Did you get their messages across as they would

have liked? Could you improve on your communication? Were they happy that you represented them accurately?

Remember that you're dealing with Spirit people who may not like you playing twenty questions with them. I always say to my students, if you'd invited a cherished guest over to your house, would you get out your clipboard and fire a list of questions at them? Of course not; you'd open a dialogue, share a conversation with them, reminisce and catch up on what they wish to share with you.

## The language of mediumship

Be mindful of the language you're using when conducting a reading, and the impression you're giving people. For example, it's far better to say 'I'm aware of ...' or 'I can hear ...' rather than 'They're telling me ...'. Your recipient might be left wondering who 'they' are – is it Spirit or is it the voices in your head!

The language you use will also serve as an indicator to you as to what psychic faculty you're using. If you hear yourself saying the words 'I think ...', then know that you've dropped out of your power and are reverting to your logical, rational, thinking mind. This usually occurs when your mind is interfering with the evidence given and you're trying to make sense of what you're perceiving. At this point you can begin to question yourself and what the evidence might mean, and self-doubt can take over, reducing your self-confidence. If in doubt, *refrain from asking questions of your sitter or audience member*; always go back to your Spirit person for further clarification.

In general, everything you say in a reading on behalf of Spirit, be it in a public forum or a private sitting, must be said with respect and dignity. If the Spirit person swears, there's no need to repeat vulgar language; rather, it can be conveyed by the statement, 'I'm aware they used colorful language in life.' However, in some instances, if you're being repeatedly impressed to use a particular colorful phrase, then pass it on, as it may be a pivotal piece of evidence that characterized the Spirit person.

During one sitting I'd linked to the grandfather of my sitter and he showed me himself opening a can of beer. I was about to pass on that information when I heard him say, 'I'm cracking a tinny', which is Australian slang for opening a can of beer. I don't generally speak in slang, but because I'd heard it distinctly I decided to pass on the information as I'd received it, namely 'He's cracking a tinny.' My client's face lit up with excitement as she told me that she was living in his house and his house was named 'Cracking a tinny'! This to me demonstrates the intelligence of the Spirit world and had I let my conscious mind interfere, this client would have missed this wonderful point of validation from her grandfather.

Finally, always speak in a confident manner that displays empathy, intelligence and benevolence to Spirit and to your sitter. Your sitter may be vulnerable, frightened or apprehensive, and this will put them at ease.

## Ethics and duty of care

We must also be very much aware of the ethics that apply when working professionally as a medium. We are, after all, dealing with people in one of the most challenging and perhaps most vulnerable times in their lives – after the death of a loved one.

Nothing can truly prepare us for death, and how we may react to death, until such time as we are confronted with it. In western culture in particular we have a fear of death in general and it is not often talked about.

I've witnessed many people trapped in the grief cycle, unable to continue with their lives as they knew it. When we're dealing with vulnerable people, we must be mindful of the messages we're bringing through and the impact those messages can have on our sitter. As mediums, we are never responsible for the actions people may take as a result of their reading, but we do have a duty of care to ensure that we do not continue a reading if the sitter is suicidal, or mentally impaired in some way, be it by grief, alcohol or drugs.

We must ensure we maintain the highest standards when reading for others. This includes checking in with our ego and ourselves. We may be tempted to corrupt our evidence in order to look good for our sitters, rather than admitting we're unable to connect with Spirit on a particular point. I've heard of many unscrupulous people who tell their sitters that they're cursed, or that their family members will not rest in peace, in order to gain financially from people's fear and grief. We also must ensure that we do not set up a cycle of dependence where we encourage the sitter to consult with us for every life decision they make. At best it is disempowering for our sitters, and at worse it is abusive of us to continue to do so.

Public demonstrations are another area in which we need to be mindful regarding what type of information is presented. What we can say in a private sitting may not apply publicly, and there are many examples that illustrate this. The most obvious ones are cases where the person in Spirit has committed atrocious acts while living, such as pedophilia or acts of violence towards children. They may have passed into the world of Spirit and wish to contact their elderly mother in the audience, perhaps to say sorry.

In such a case, it's not necessary to describe exactly what he did in front of everyone, but we can certainly bring his apology to the mother's attention in a respectful and tactful way, thereby sparing her unnecessary trauma, shame and grief. You might compare the medium's approach to revealing information to a physician's Hippocratic Oath, whereby they vow to 'do no harm' whenever possible.

**Exercises**

1. Practice sitting in the power two or three times a week. Get to know your main Spirit guide and have a chat with them regarding your readings. Get their advice on how you conducted your reading and how you might improve in the future.
2. Practice the language of mediumship. Eliminate 'I think' from your vocabulary and replace it with terms such as 'I know', 'I feel', 'I sense' or 'I hear'. Align your language to the psychic faculties you're employing during contact.
3. Invite volunteer sitters in to have a private sitting or mini-demonstration and then ask for feedback.
4. Hone your craft and practice at local psychic fairs, etc.

CHAPTER 10

# Public demonstrations

*'We convince by our presence.'*
*~ Walt Whitman*

P ublic demonstrations are a way for mediums to connect with a larger community base and showcase the fact that *love is eternal* and that *we survive beyond the physical body*. People who perhaps would not normally be open to receiving a private reading may be reached in a public demonstration. It's often the case that the non-believer or skeptic who's dragged along to such an event will receive contact from the Spirit world. The look of amazement or even shock on their faces is priceless.

In a public setting it's important to remember that you're only as good as your audience. In other words, if your audience is flat then your energy will also be flat, leading to uninspiring communication with Spirit. It is vitally important that you develop your unique brand of showmanship, to keep the audience interested, animated and stimulated. Your audience effectively becomes your battery pack and it's important for them to be as excited as possible.

When standing up in front of an audience, tell them and act as if you're excited to be there; convey this via your spoken word, your posture and your energy. Playing evocative music or giving an inspirational speech before the readings is a good way to raise the energy in the room. This, of course, depends on the type of demonstration you're holding and your own unique approach. If you're running your own event you might choose music that is modern or upbeat in order to get the audience in the right mood. In a Spiritualist church environment, a hymn may be more appropriate.

Music is highly evocative and filled with meaning. I usually wake up to a song playing in my head that I will then play later at the demonstration. The song I play is always significant to a contact I make during the demonstration and often sets the tone or mood. Sometimes the songs are humorous, other times somber, but they're always relevant.

It's important to let the audience members know how you work and that a recipient's response is what mediums rely on to make and keep the contact. Tell them before you start that you require, for example, a loud, audible 'Yes' if they can understand the information, a 'No' if they can't, and a 'Don't know' if they're unsure.

Why do we ask for this feedback? Two reasons: it keeps the whole audience engaged as they listen to the responses of the recipient, and it establishes an energetic link between the medium and the recipient.

Resist the temptation to have your recipient give you information beyond a simple 'Yes' or 'No'. You'll need to be in control of this and try to discourage a dialogue developing with audience members or the public demonstration will quickly become like a private sitting. Your conscious mind will engage and weaken your link to Spirit as you try to color what you're receiving with what the recipient is telling you. At worst, you'll lose your connection and focus on Spirit and start reading the recipient psychically. This will have a flow-on effect in that the rest of the audience will lose interest and the energy in the room will start to drop.

Start a demonstration with a contact at the rear of the room if possible, so that you're able to harness the power and energy of all the audience members present. This is not always in your control as Spirit may choose a person in the front; however, if you're working collaboratively with your Spirit team you can request that the first contact is always at the rear of the room.

Be aware of where you're standing on the platform and what your energy is doing. If the recipient is on the left-hand side of the room, for example, make sure you stand on the right-hand side so that, once again, all the audience is included. Remember to maintain eye contact with the whole audience, not just the person the message is for.

When conducting a public demonstration (or indeed a private sitting), remember to keep the power moving. Develop techniques to move the power within you so that you can sustain it for the duration of the contact. What I mean by keeping the power moving is that while demonstrating you move around the stage to keep the flow of energy going. Through keeping the power moving you'll go deeper into the information and the quality of evidence will be increased. If you feel yourself losing the power, pause, take a sip of water and reconnect before you proceed. Have a joke or two up your sleeve so that you can elicit a laugh from the audience. Have a little banter with them, but remember to be true to you.

Stay open-minded. The power keeps moving and building with an open mind, rather than an analytical mind. An analytical mind will want to be prescriptive, focusing on defining features such as looks and height without touching the soul of the Spirit person. Most importantly, if the power is fully developed you don't have to interpret information. It will simply *manifest*. Your delivery will flow effortlessly and the number of pauses between receiving information will sharply diminish.

When conducting a reading make a commitment to the information you've received and follow through with your reading. Your commitment should always be to the Spirit world first and foremost, not to the audience. There will always be audience members who are desperate to hear from their loved ones and will try to make your evidence fit. Don't be swayed by the audience; commit to your person in the Spirit world. Stay with them until your evidence makes sense to your recipient.

To illustrate what I mean by making a commitment to Spirit, I offer this example. If you state that you have a girl here, in her teens, with long, sandy hair, whose name is Chris and someone in the audience says, 'I have a son called Chris with long hair', don't change the sex of your person to make it fit. If you felt a girl, stay with that and keep talking to your Spirit person until you can connect her with her loved ones.

By making this commitment you will assure people of your credibility and will gain the confidence of not only the audience but the world of Spirit too. Your language should be confident and definite. Saying 'I *think* I have your aunty' does not inspire confidence. You shouldn't 'think', you should *know*; either you have the aunty or you do not. If you don't know then don't guess; keep working with the Spirit person until you do know.

There will be occasions when audience members will want to direct the evidence or reading given. They may be expecting to hear a particular word or phrase, or to hear from a particular person. If an audience member asks you for particular information, it's important to convey to that person that as mediums we work for and on behalf of the Spirit world. Gently remind the person that if you start interacting with them, then you're by default not working with their loved one. You may find also that you'll fall out of the power as your mental mind becomes engaged and tries to make the evidence fit with what the recipient is telling you. This will at the very least dilute your evidence and at the very worst corrupt it.

Have prearranged cues that you've agreed on with your Spirit team that will allow you to flow in your delivery of information when in contact with Spirit. These cues might be 'Your mother tells me ...', 'Your brother shows me ...' or 'Grandmother is making me aware that ...'. These cues will allow you to catch your breath briefly while the next piece of information is being delivered to you to pass on.

It can be useful to sit with Spirit days or even a week or two ahead of your scheduled public demonstration and work out with Spirit how you would like the event to be. Discuss how you'd like the evidence to be delivered and what type of evidence you'd like to showcase. What type of contacts would you like to have and is there a particular theme to the event? This will give Spirit the opportunity, well in advance, to ready themselves for your demonstration so that it flows much more smoothly for you. This process will calm your nerves as it allows you to feel in control. Having said this, try to let go and have no expectations on the day. By having no expectations you are allowing the magic of mediumship to manifest as Spirit feels best.

Similarly, it is highly useful for your mediumship development and refinement to once again sit with your Spirit guide *after your event*, to debrief on how you went. It's useful at this time to evaluate your communication and to ask your guide how it can be improved upon in the future.

As for an individual reading, reconnect with your Spirit contacts from your event and ask for feedback, in much the same way as you'd seek feedback in an employee appraisal session. Find out from them whether you got their messages across as they would have liked. Did you represent them accurately? Could you have done better?

Keep most readings at around the seven to eight minute mark before moving on to another contact. Towards the beginning of your development you'll find that you become so comfortable in a good contact that you'll be reluctant to move on to another. It's important to develop the confidence to leave a good contact and move to another contact, in order to keep the demonstration dynamic. In a public forum there will be many people who are hoping to hear from their loved ones and therefore the aim is to make as many connections as possible.

# Stagecraft

As you become more confident and proficient with your mediumship, don't forget to also develop your *stagecraft* – the way in which you skillfully and competently use the power and keep the audience engaged. This will become a signature style that sets you apart from others.

Remember to always be in control and to maintain your dignity; you're an ambassador for the Spirit world. Be mindful of your language and the way you conduct yourself on stage. Don't be afraid to change your presentation style to suit each situation you're demonstrating in.

Never underestimate the intelligence of the Spirit world; even today it continues to amaze me. Over the years I've found that in demonstrations Spirit will often produce themes in the messages given that are relevant for all the audience members. The words and messages given during a demonstration may contain a phrase or word that someone other than the intended recipient might also be looking for as a verification that their loved one is also present.

I recall during one public demonstration, a gentleman from the world of Spirit made contact and immediately showed me his hands covered in grease. I gave this evidence to his wife in the audience, stating that although his hands were covered in grease I knew that he didn't work with his hands but was in fact a musician. What I didn't know at the time was that the wife had written to her husband in her journal some weeks earlier, telling him she'd be attending my upcoming demonstration. She'd never seen a medium before and wasn't even sure that the afterlife existed, although she hoped it did. She told her husband that if he was indeed with her as she was writing, she'd give him a code word and if the medium (me in this case) gave her the code word, she'd be convinced that he was around her.

Her code word, of course, was 'grease' and she'd even written and outlined in her journal: 'Grease is the word'. She was a fan of the movie and the musical *Grease*, so this was very meaningful to her. You can imagine her delight and relief when I said I could see his hands covered in grease! She contacted me for a private sitting some weeks later and bought her journal with her to show me the entry. Of course, she'd also come up with a code word for that sitting and once again her husband did not let her down.

This was a wonderful confirmation for her that the love they shared was eternal and it gave her comfort as she moved through her grieving process. Not all Spirit contacts will respond in code, and nor should we expect them to, but for this woman it was her validation.

## Simultaneous contacts

When demonstrating, there will be times when two (or more in some cases) people in Spirit will make contact at the same time. The reason this occurs is because both Spirit people will have similar energies, be similar in personality or have similar roles, such as being a grandmother.

A skilled medium needs to be aware when this occurs and take charge of the situation by separating the two personalities and dealing with them one at a time. From the audience perspective this can be a great situation to witness if it's handled exceptionally by the medium.

I had this occur during a mother's day demonstration, where a woman in the audience had both grandmothers appear at the same time. I had to separate the grandmothers out and then work with each one separately. I bounced between the two, getting two to three statements from one before switching to the other, then bringing them back together for the message that was about the love they had for their granddaughter. It was a beautiful connection for the recipient, as she truly felt the love in that moment.

## Handle the noes

In a public demonstration it can be a highly stressful experience when your recipient is constantly shaking their head or saying no to the evidence you're presenting. The only way to overcome this is to have complete trust and faith in the Spirit world. They'll never get it wrong and will never let you down. They have a vested interest, after all, in making contact and reaching their loved ones.

If you get a 'No', it can be very easy to lose confidence when you're on stage. The key here is to stay in your power and keep going back to Spirit for further information or clarification. *Be bold and back yourself.* Never assume you're wrong just because you get a 'No'; I love the noes and will persist until I get the results.

During one demonstration I gave with a mother's day theme I brought through two brothers who'd both died in motorbike incidents. I kept directing the evidence to a recipient and she kept looking at me and saying 'No'. She couldn't take the evidence and the contact. I knew I was with this woman, but she kept saying 'No'. Any professional working medium will tell you that meeting blank faces on your first contact of the day can be enough to knock your confidence flat.

I moved on to my next contact but still had the brothers with me. During the intermission the woman asked me if she had to know the people in Spirit. When I said 'No, you might know *of* them', she said she could place the brothers. They were her mother-in-law's sons, who she'd never met.

Continuing with the second half of my demonstration I was able to bring through further information that this woman was able to acknowledge and pass on to their mother, even though the mother was not present. It was such a powerful moment and transformed an audience that might have been sitting on the fence to one that was totally convinced of the intelligence and existence of the Spirit world.

Remember: be persistent in how you handle the noes. Sometimes people in a large audience don't have the confidence to speak when they're singled out, or they can get stage fright and have a momentary lapse in memory. These are common scenarios and it's not unusual for an audience member to approach a medium after an event and confirm a contact. Never assume you were wrong. Be prepared to be wrong, but work with your team to improve your trust and confidence.

**Exercises**

1. Connect to your Spirit team. Set your intention for the demonstration: how do you wish it to unfold? What type of contacts would you like? Will there be a theme to the messages? A caution: don't be so rigid that you're unable to work if Spirit decides to work differently than the way you've agreed.

2. Develop a playlist of power songs that you can listen to when preparing for your demonstration that energizes and inspires you.

3. Develop an evocative playlist of songs to use during your demonstration that will inspire or evoke an emotional response in your audience.

4. Define prearranged cues with the Spirit world that allows them to fill in the blanks for you. For example 'Your father tells me …' – then allow Spirit to insert what they wish to say. This technique is great to keep the flow going.

5. Enroll in a public speaking course to hone your presentation abilities and refine your stagecraft.

6. Film yourself and critique your posture, portioning and speaking voice with the aim of improving your presentation. Remember not to be overly critical of yourself.

CHAPTER 11

# The importance of self-care

*'Self-care is a priority and a necessity, not a luxury, in the work we do.' ~ Unknown*

elf-care is an aspect of mediumship that is often overlooked by both developing and professional mediums. It's very easy to get carried away with the idea of being of service to others. Without self-awareness, however, the risk is neglect and possibly harm to yourself. Quite frankly, it isn't wise to serve others when there's a negative cost to you and to your health. This is a very important point to embrace. If you're running on empty, your mediumship, by default, will also suffer.

Mediums are born sensitive and will struggle to live with this sensitivity all of their lives. As a result, their lifestyle choices, knowingly or unknowingly, may cause them to develop health disorders and conditions related to stress. The most common that I've witnessed (some of which I've also experienced) include:

- chronic fatigue
- fibromyalgia
- IBS
- food intolerances

- food allergies
- adrenal exhaustion
- poor or disrupted sleep
- nervousness
- stress
- anxiety disorders
- chronic pain
- sensitivity to light and loud noises.

Not surprisingly, the topic of self-care is highly pertinent to the developing medium.

Self-care, in my opinion, can only be put into practice when *self-worth* is present. Take a moment and say the word 'self-worth' out loud and notice what feeling arises in your body. What's your reaction to these words? What can you feel deep inside yourself? Do you feel stress and tension, particularly in your stomach area? Do any emotions or thoughts come to mind? Take note of your feelings as a passive observer, without judging what you encounter. If you're unable to look at yourself in the mirror and say aloud 'I love you' without averting your eyes, then know that you have work to do on self-worth.

The first step in engaging in the work of self-care is to recognize that improvement is needed. Once this is acknowledged, it's a matter of being open and committed to the stages of healing that will naturally come your way, be that medical, physical, emotional or Spiritual in nature. Again, bear in mind that your type of sensitivity and your way of addressing it is unique to you. Each person's journey of self-worth is a one-of-a-kind experience that follows their soul's blueprint – the plan that the Divine Architect has set out for you.

Many mediums do lead quite stressful and challenging lives from a very young age. When I sat with Spirit on this very topic, I was made aware that these life experiences were essentially a kind of training ground so that the medium could *graduate* with real experiential knowledge of the human condition, including suffering. Armed with this first-hand knowledge they are ideally placed to be able to respond with empathy and understanding not only to those in the incarnated state but also to those who have crossed into the world of Spirit. There's tremendous healing power when you're able to look into someone's eyes and say, 'I get you, I feel your pain. I've been where you are.' Of course, merely saying this kind of thing is not enough. For our work to be authentic, it must be based on experience, not theory.

On a practical level, there are many things we can do to create good self-care routines in our lives. I've outlined below the ones that I feel are the most important.

## Getting good-quality sleep

The first thing I teach my students and clients is to get their sleep right as a foundational and critical step to self-care. Sleep hygiene is essential for optimal health of mind, body and Spirit, for it is in the deep sleep state that repair work is achieved. Lack of good quality sleep is the basis of many health conditions, and in some cases it may even cause health issues that can lead to death.

Anything you can do to ensure good quality sleep will serve you well, personally and professionally. If you're getting adequate, quality, restful sleep, then you're best equipped to get through your day as a sensitive.

I've had many developing mediums say to me that they can't get to sleep at night because Spirit is waking them up. It's not Spirit that's waking them up; rather, they're listening and searching for Spirit even in the sleep state. This can certainly be true in the initial development stage, where we're excited to make contact so are continuously looking for Spirit. Spirit will respect our earthly need for rest and privacy. They will not interrupt us if we don't wish them to do so. Let Spirit know that you don't wish to be disturbed in your sleep unless it is for an emergency. Then be mindful that *you* stick to your request, as Spirit most definitely will!

Practicing a good night-time routine is a must and can encompass the following:

- **Switch off from electronic media** – switch to flight mode so that you're not being interrupted by incoming text messages or emails. Better still, place your devices in another room.
- **Sleep in a dark room** – keep your bedroom as dark as possible (total blackout is best). Use a sleep eye mask to ensure this if window coverings aren't adequate. Light will disrupt your production of the sleep hormone melatonin.
- **Keep cool** – keep your bedroom slightly on the cool side so that you're not overheating in your sleep, and waking up. Don't overdo it, though – the same applies if you're too cold.
- **Minimize clutter** – keep your bedside tables and room clutter-free so that your mind isn't distracted before sleep.
- **Use neutral bedding** – sleep in bedding that is restful, using calming colors such as blues, turquoise or whites.
- **Apply sleep remedies** – use magnesium or natural sleep remedies, if required, to ensure you get to sleep and stay asleep.
- **Minimize caffeine** – minimize stimulating beverages at night, such as caffeine-based drinks. This also applies to alcohol.

These are all simple strategies that you may already be aware of, yet few of us are disciplined enough to put them into place.

## Maintaining boundaries

The key to maintaining an energetic equilibrium is to set boundaries and stick with them. Be realistic about what you can handle, taking into consideration your own unique characteristics, energy levels, lifestyle, family responsibilities, and preferences. Honor and protect your need for down time and allow others to do the same. Interestingly, enforcing our own boundaries is at times more difficult than asking others to respect them! The temptation to push just a little further can be hard to resist. It is a true adage that *we teach others how to treat us by the way we treat ourselves.*

I've seen many budding mediums and even professional mediums making the mistake of constantly being *on*, giving readings wherever they go and in any situation they may find themselves in. They seem not to have developed an off switch – a vitally important tool for every medium. Without an off switch, a medium's energy becomes drained and the quality of their readings diminishes.

Keep in mind that you're not obligated to be constantly available to those who need help, any more than a person in any other field of work is. Your energy is your prime mediumship tool of the trade and it should be nourished, protected, fiercely guarded and used responsibly.

Your mediumship ability should also not be used like a cheap party trick and you should never feel you have to perform, to prove you have ability. I'd be rich indeed if I had a dollar for every time I was out and someone exclaimed, 'Oh, are you a medium? What can you see for me?' Can you imagine if I was at a party and found out someone was a hair stylist? I'd never ask if that person would mind trimming my hair at the party, to prove that they were a genuine hair stylist! In the same way, if I met an accountant socially, I wouldn't start downloading my latest profit and loss statement on my smartphone and ask them to review my figures. Yet I've seen so many mediums or psychics feel they have to prove themselves on the spot, depleting their energy as they give in to their egos. The medium's ability needs to be respected like any other profession or job. That respect starts with us. We must learn how to communicate our boundaries kindly and firmly.

An interesting observation from my healing practice is that people who don't have healthy boundaries will usually have leaky gut issues. The gut's boundary, being the gut lining, is breached – a physical representation of what's going on energetically for the person. Similarly, a lack of healthy boundaries is also indicated in people who have autoimmune issues. Our immune system is designed to keep pathogens or invaders out. When pathogens overrun our system or breach our defenses, we suffer ill health. These pathogens can be an invader such as a fungus, a bacteria or a virus, or an energetic invader such as an abuse intent, where inappropriate conduct carried out by a perpetrator leaves behind an energy signature that says, 'I have no defenses.'

If you're suffering from gut or autoimmune issues then you can be confident that addressing boundary issues will help alleviate these health symptoms. Any work where you're consciously strengthening your boundaries will serve you well by improving and strengthening your energy and, simultaneously, your mediumship. Remember that the quality of your mediumship is directly related to the quality of your energy. You can work day and night on the mechanics of mediumship, but if your energy isn't stable, the results you achieve will be inconsistent. The same is actually true for all aspects of our lives, both personal and professional. Everything begins and ends with energy, for it is the quality of vibration that determines our essence, that part of us that defines our individuality.

## Keeping unhealthy ego in check

Ego can be of two kinds, healthy or unhealthy. A healthy ego is that necessary part of our psyche that drives us to continuously improve and to better ourselves. One of its main functions is to keep us safe and give us definition and direction. An unhealthy ego, on the other hand, is a perspective on self that is out of balance. This ego leads one into all kinds of confusion and difficulties. I wish to speak here about how an unhealthy ego can affect the work of a medium.

There are a lot of would-be mediums who genuinely believe that they have ability when they don't. You'll find them on a lot of online forums fiercely pushing their viewpoints on how things should or should not be done. During public demonstrations, they'll claim to be mediums when they are actually working psychically, without the presence of Spirit being evident. They take great delight in critiquing and judging other mediums' ability and style. They'll talk with authority even though they may never have conducted a professional reading or put any of the knowledge they're discussing into practice.

At best, these people are simply misinformed, and at worst they can cause serious damage to another's confidence and development. These individuals may start to move into the dangerous world of self-delusion, thinking they are the next messiahs. It's a slippery slope from this state of mind into a power trip. Many find themselves thriving on the fact that they're holding power over people. They may use their influence to scare their targets with nonsense, for example telling people they're cursed or that they have attachments on them.

With Spirit, there is no comparison of self or others and certainly no fearful statements concerning curses or the like. If you find yourself hearing things like this or thinking about them yourself, back off and return to the basics of your Spiritual education: humility, gratitude, fearlessness, kindness, compassion and love. Always strive to be of service with an open and loving heart. Focus inward on self and how you can best serve the Spirit world. Above all, keep your ego in check.

It doesn't matter what others are doing – that's their business and they're following their own path. What does matter is that you are following *your* own path, the one that Spirit is guiding you to pursue. Don't let fame or notoriety go to your head – strive to serve with humility. My definition of humility is acknowledging that you are no more and certainly no less than anyone else. It may help to remind yourself that growth is eternal and no matter what you experience or learn, there's always someone who's wiser and more developed than you. If you keep this understanding in the forefront of your mind while enacting Spiritual service, it can help you walk that line between humility and pride.

My mother gave me some words of wisdom at a very young age that have served me well over the years. She said to never assume you know it all; even if you think you know, say you don't and let others give you their take on things. You may just learn something that you've never considered before, or come to see something from a different perspective.

Be open to continuous learning. Be prepared to be wrong, and if you are, rejoice in the fact that you're now able to correct something in yourself. Remain open, yet also hopeful and confident in your ability. Develop critical discrimination skills – whatever you do must feel right for you. Don't give your power away, and use discernment while being willing to ask questions and to research further.

## Managing stress

Generally speaking, stress is the biggest cause of energy depletion. As mentioned earlier, energy management is a must for mediums since our energy quality directly impacts the quality of our mediumship. Therefore, minimizing the effects of stress on our lives is a priority.

The first step in stress management is to determine how much stress you have in your life. The stress in your life may be broadly categorized into two areas: stressors that you can change and stressors that you can't change due to circumstances.

Make a list of your stressors, placing each in the appropriate category. Your goal is to then conduct an honest appraisal of each item on the list, asking yourself, 'Am I really stuck with this stressor due to circumstances, or is there another way?' This process may take a while and your perspective may change even as you work on the lists, so be ready to adapt your thinking as your viewpoints shift! Once you're comfortable with your lists, make it a priority to work through them to determine ways to eliminate or reduce the impact of each stressor. Remind yourself along the way that often it is our *mindset* about our circumstances rather than the circumstances themselves that needs to change when we start to reframe our stressors.

If finances are the main cause of stress in your life, then be open enough to enlist the help of a skillful budget advisor when necessary, whether this is someone you know or someone you hire. There is much to learn about financial planning, and if you approach it with an attitude of hope and determination, you can structure a much more secure and peaceful life for yourself and those you love. So often our finances are ruled by the fears and myths we've taken on throughout life. Shine the light of clarity and information upon this subject, understanding that Spirituality encompasses everything, including the way we handle finances. There's nothing inherently wrong with money; it's the misuse of it, and the false ideas people have about it, that puts them in a negative relationship with their economic life. I encourage you to take a fresh look at this matter and get excited about establishing a positive relationship with your finances. Learn to see your financial health as a wonderful part of your self-care routine and your self-worth development. This includes allowing yourself to take a holiday, or at least mini-breaks, from time to time. You can create a low-cost mini holiday for yourself by taking a day to relax in nature and share laughter with a friend. You may have to change some of your descriptions of what a pleasurable day consists of, but the truth is that these things – Nature and friendship – are the finest the world has to offer.

Sometimes an inability to trust others and relinquish control holds us back from taking care of our own needs. For example, in order to save money as a single parent I found myself compressing my working day to ensure I could manage a school pick-up and drop-off. I then tried to fit in cleaning, cooking and working on the administration of my business. The result was that I completely exhausted myself. I realized that this was not going to be sustainable in the long run, since my energy levels were constantly being depleted and, as with so many people who wear too many hats, nothing was being done well or to completion. It felt like everything was partially finished, leaving me feeling frustrated, guilty, and unfulfilled.

After taking stock of my situation, I took the decision to employ cleaners to clean my home, a nanny to collect my child from school and an assistant to manage my appointments. When I did this, I discovered that my productivity increased, my health improved and my energy levels stabilized. I felt lighter and more in tune with Spirit and I was able to be a better parent to my child because I could be fully present with her during our time together. The irony was that the employment of my support team did not negatively impact my bottom line. In fact, the reverse was true – my annual turnover increased by 25 per cent. The flow of this dynamic had such a positive impact in my life in so many ways. I was able to make time to go to the gym and I began to develop my *resilience network*: a team of people around me who were supporting my health and wellbeing goals. I have now become the biggest fan of outsourcing, and encourage you to consider it as an option.

Financial stress is one of the biggest zappers of energy, so I must say here that if you find your mediumship work is too difficult to maintain for financial reasons, it's perfectly okay to step away from it in order to earn enough to support your family. There are times in our lives where so much turmoil and angst is going on that it becomes prudent to put mediumship on hold for a time. Our stressors may be health-related, financial or relationship-related. Mediums have personal lives as well, and can experience difficulties like anyone else, such as the breakdown of a marriage or a death in the family. Being a medium does not make one immune to grief. It is only right to give yourself the time you need to cope with the ups and downs of life, just as you would advise anyone else to do. Remember, you are not a machine, but a living, breathing human being, and you must be as kind and gentle to yourself as you strive to be to others. Never be afraid to give yourself permission to put yourself first and take a sabbatical from the Spirit world. They will understand and will be waiting for you if and when you decide to return.

Another area of life that can bring us various levels of stress – and in some instances the greatest stress of all – is our personal relationships with family and friends. A Spiritual path is sometimes seen as a path free of normal human struggles, but this is not true. If you're one of those people who are not living the 'Hallmark card' ideal family dream, then join the club, for you are most likely in the majority. In spite of the ups and downs of our personal lives, it's important to remember that we are all born into our *perfect* birth families and life conditions, even if we forget this at times. What do I mean by perfect? I mean that the situations we are born into will support our life purpose perfectly, even if we can't appreciate it at the time.

When you combine all the stressors, you may find there's a great deal to navigate in life. So what's the best way to do so? In the first instance, I believe we need to work on ourselves, letting go of the idea that we are somehow responsible for other people's life choices or reactions. What others think of us is none of our business. What *is* our business is living life as authentically as we can and leading a life that supports our life purpose and passions. Sometimes the most loving thing you can do for yourself is to walk away from family and/or friends, especially if the relationships are toxic. Don't feel guilty for doing this; your health and stability must always be made a priority. Think of someone trying to save a person who's drowning – if they jump into the water without support, the panicked swimmer can pull them under. If they stand on the shore and throw the person a life ring, or go to help them with a life jacket on, they can save the person without endangering themselves.

If you're finding stressors are impacting your ability to connect to Spirit, then consider taking time to work out a solution to the issues, even if this means taking a break from mediumship. Your family and Spirit will be grateful for your decision, and, most importantly, you'll have the time you need to stabilize yourself.

# Good nutrition

In traditional Chinese medicine, there's a belief that our energy comes from three sources: the life force energy, or *chi*, that we're born with; the chi that comes from the breath we inhale; and the chi that we obtain from the food we eat.

It's no coincidence that meditation and focusing on the breath is an integral part of mediumship development. Food is also a component that should not be overlooked, particularly if you're working as a medium and are motivated to bring the best of you to your work.

My personal approach to nutrition is to learn to tune into your body and understand what it's asking for so that you can eat what your body needs. There are a lot of diets based on various philosophies; some are fads and others require lifestyle changes. The key is to understand your own body's requirements and then stick to that. Also, be aware that these requirements will change throughout your lifetime, depending on your age, circumstances, gender and thought patterns, so try to remain adaptable. What you are eating should increase your energy and keep you feeling light, alert and content. If you're eating foods that make your system sluggish, tired, and depleted then you're doing yourself a disservice.

In my own journey I've found that as I've grown Spiritually my food choices have changed. My sensitivity to chemicals, hormones and other additives has increased, so I make a conscious choice to choose organic foods where possible. Whatever eating choices you make, ensure that you choose food of the highest energetic quality you can find. I encourage you to examine your relationship with food. Are you an emotional eater? Are there other triggers that determine your eating choices? Do you make time to adequately nourish your body? Do you take the time to lovingly enjoy food or do you race through life with the attitude that stopping to eat is an inconvenience?

Having a loving relationship with the food you eat will generate vitality, which will permeate every cell of your body. This in turn will influence your mental health and your general perspective on life.

## Drugs and alcohol

It goes without saying that if you are drug or alcohol impaired, you should not be conducting mediumship readings. At times of stress, it's easy for people to reach for that drink or to partake in recreational drugs. These substances, however, will depress your energy reserves and will have an impact on your emotional and mental faculties.

It's through the mind that mediumship is facilitated; therefore, if your mind is impaired in some way, the quality of your mediumship will suffer. As I've noted previously, mediumship carries certain responsibilities. Keeping our minds and bodies in balance is certainly one of them. If you have an issue with drugs or alcohol, take the high road and back off from the work until you've dealt with it. Spirit will be supportive of your recovery and grateful that you've chosen to act with integrity and honor.

I recall witnessing one medium that was bipolar and in need of medication to address the issue but was not taking the medication to stabilize herself. She was using aggressive language in her work with clients, and projecting her own issues onto them. The clients were left feeling energetically assaulted and not inspired in any way. We all know that the aim of a good, quality mediumship reading is to leave your client hopeful, inspired and uplifted. If anything other than this is occurring, take the time to examine your habits to see if alcohol or drugs might be a contributing factor.

This industry is not regulated, making self-regulation imperative. We must always bear in mind that we are representatives of the industry, and our actions reflect upon other mediums. Pledge to yourself to always work with integrity and full self-awareness, developing the maturity and honesty necessary to know when to take a sabbatical from the work, and when to embrace it fully.

## Self-awareness

Awareness of your own strengths and weaknesses is a must; no one knows you better than you. As mentioned in Chapter 6, 'Overcoming barriers to mediumship', to be the best medium you can be it's necessary to understand the ebbs and flows of your own energy; it's important that you don't allow your energy to become depleted. Keeping a journal of your energy levels will also alert you to how and when you do your best work. Are you brighter and lighter during summer? Do you work better in the mornings? Monitor and track yourself over the days, the weeks, the months and the year to gauge when is the best time for your readings, workshops, retreats, or other kinds of service.

Once you have this insight into your energy levels, you can plan and coordinate your mediumship to suit. For example, my energy is much more expansive in the spring, so this is the time that I schedule more public demonstrations. During the winter months I am more inwardly focused, so I like to do all my writing during those months.

Self-awareness also applies to your internal world. Be attuned to your inner Spirit and find out how it wishes to work with you. You may find that your inner Spirit is guiding you to avoid certain situations, people or types of work, just as it guides you to interact with other people and places. Trust your intuition and your observations of both yourself and others.

The more self-aware you become, the more easily your life will flow. When you're fully in tune with your identity and how your soul wishes you to operate in the world, you will find yourself most at peace with your vocation and lifestyle.

## Energy clearing

As mediums, the more deeply we develop, the greater our sensitivity becomes. Consequently, developing a disciplined approach to energy clearing is a must. There are various techniques you can use to clear and protect your energy from other influences, but I've chosen a fundamental three-step approach, outlined here:

### 1. Clear your energy

Clear your energy by calling upon Archangel Michael and affirm the following: 'Archangel Michael, I ask that any and all energies that I have absorbed that are not my own be removed and cleared now. I thank you.' Wait for a moment, and then affirm, 'I am clear at all times; I only hold onto my own energy.'

### 2. Cleanse your energy

Visualize yourself as a clear vessel, as if your body were made of glass. Then imagine an infinite supply of liquid gold light (or any other color that makes you happy) being poured through the crown of your head, and keep pouring until you are completely filled with light, allowing all darkness to spill over and into the ground. Then allow this gold light to overflow so that you are cocooned in an egg-shaped bubble of light.

### 3. Protect your energy

Ask Archangel Michael to place his wings of protection around you, keeping you safe at all times.

In an emergency situation, such as a toxic or hostile environment, you may wish to imagine that you're wearing a skin-tight black wetsuit that covers your entire body except for your eyes. Then imagine that the inside of your wetsuit is filled with golden light, then also add pink, loving light into the suit. Know that you are safe and that no negative energies will be able to penetrate the suit.

## Protection from Spirit?

If you are fearful, neurotic or believe that when opening yourself to the world of Spirit you are at risk from *entities, evil Spirits* or *possessions*, then I would advise against embarking on a mediumship development path. Your mind is a powerful tool and a necessary component of mediumship development and communication. An undisciplined mind can at best make you question your sanity and at worse deliver a mental breakdown. Fear in an undisciplined or unstable mind can manifest a reality that may not be pleasant.

For this reason, I personally do not believe that any form of protection from Spirit contacts is necessary. On the contrary, if you're of sound mind, have strong mental discipline and know the world of Spirit intimately, you know that you are *unable* to be harmed by Spirit. The only protection I believe is required – which I've outlined above – is protection from other living people! We have more to fear from those in the land of the living than from those in the world of Spirit.

My main guide gave me wonderful advice early in my development when I questioned the need for protection when working with Spirit. His response was, 'If there is darkness, you simply turn on the light.' This statement, delivered in a calm, matter-of-fact, neutral way, was very profound for me as it highlighted that it is our irrational, emotive mind that will give in to fear-based thinking.

Of course, mental illness will impact your ability to be rational and in control of your mental faculties. If you're suffering from mental illness, there's no reason for shame. Many of us go through periods of life when mental illness strikes, and there are treatments available. As with other stressors in life, it's best that you refrain from any mediumship development until you're well recovered. Never fear, Spirit will be standing by.

## Life–work balance

Getting the life–work balance right is imperative for all mediums, but especially so for those who are working in the field professionally. You'll notice that I use the term 'life–work balance' rather than the generally accepted 'work–life balance'. I've done this to emphasize the important fact that we're here to *live* our lives; we're not here just to work.

As with much about mediumship, there's no one-size-fits-all formula for life–work balance. I would, however, encourage you to explore this, to discover the balance that works for you and your family. As working mediums, if we don't get this right our relationships suffer, our health suffers, our bodies become depleted, we lose passion for Spirit and for the work, and we may become resentful of anyone who demands our attention and time.

Mediums must always schedule time in their working week to have mini-breaks that have nothing to do with Spirituality and everything to do with resting and restoring their own soul and Spirit. Take time to have FUN. Choose activities that are fun for you and bring you happiness and contentment. It's important not to let our professional practice with Spirit cause us to lose sight of earthly pleasures. Take a new cooking class, go dancing or learn a new skill such as pottery. Cultivate friendships with people from all walks of life so that you can maintain a balanced perspective.

## Exercises

1. Sleep hygiene – as outlined above, ensure that you get at least 8 hours of good-quality deep sleep. Use a sleep app if you find it helpful. Make sure your bedroom is darkened and that you stick to a regular routine.

2. Energy hygiene – practice the techniques I have outlined above, in the section 'Energy clearing'.

3. Magnesium – consult with a naturopath and ensure you are getting adequate amounts of magnesium to counter the effects of stress on the body.

4. Say no to things you don't want to do or are unable to do. Practice saying 'No' without the need to elaborate or to provide reasons or excuses.

5. Build up your resilience network, including representation from both professional and personal networks. Make sure that they are people you can trust and who you know have your back.

6. Close your eyes and observe how you're feeling. Do you note any discomfort, nausea, aches, pains, or anything else? Now clear your energy by calling upon Archangel Michael and affirming the following: 'Archangel Michael, I ask that any and all energies that I have absorbed that are not my own be removed and cleared now, and I thank you.' Check in again. Has anything changed for you?

7. Keep your energy bright, clear and strong at all times by practicing energy work such as tai chi, yoga, martial arts, meditation, qi gong and reiki.

8. Eat a healthy, balanced diet that suits your body and your lifestyle. Choose clean and organic foods where possible.

9. Try something new and unrelated to your Spiritual work to give yourself a chance to rebalance. Choose activities that place you in nature, be it at the beach or in a forest.

CHAPTER 12

# Student and mentor

*'What is a teacher? I'll tell you: it isn't someone who teaches
something, but someone who inspires the student to give of her
best in order to discover what she already knows.'*
*~ Paulo Coelho, The Witch of Portobello*

I am of the personal belief that the *teacher* resides within our own soul and is already part of us. Our soul has been teaching us from the very moment we were born. Our biggest challenge is to recognize the teacher within and then to have the courage and fortitude to put the teachings of our own soul into daily practice.

Some believe that a teacher's role is to instruct you on a process or methodology and to essentially pass on information. This can be useful for teaching certain things, such as how to drive a car or cook a meal, but it has limitations. This is especially true when the teacher teaches according to a standard curriculum or set structure without tailoring the instruction to the needs of the individual, to highlight their strengths, natural ability and interests.

Many teachers will say 'This is how it's always been taught' as they cling to a process or method that may not have any relevance in our current epoch. Although it's useful at times to honor tradition, in doing so we may run the risk of limiting growth and innovation.

Teachers who are unable to teach beyond tradition risk becoming stagnant and irrelevant.

In making this statement I'm not disregarding traditions, since they're a fundamental part of our knowledge base. What I'm saying is that we need to keep open minds so that we don't miss out on innovations and new information that comes to hand.

A mentor is a different story. A mentor strives to embody the true meaning of the word 'educate', which comes from the Latin word *educare* – 'to lead'. I believe a mentor's role is to lead the student forth into new territory where the wisdom that is already inherent within them may rise up into their conscious mind. A mentor must meet you where you are, recognize your abilities, and then impart the tools and wisdom that allow you to access those abilities yourself. In other words, they must be able to show you the window but not tell you what to see.

Remember, your soul is eternal and will contain memory of all the lifetimes you've lived, where all your intuitive and mediumistic ability has been honed. It's from this wealth of memory, this data repository, housed within your soul that your true teachings are accessed. Your soul blends and joins your Spirit team, who then continue to awaken, hone, and further develop your ability in this current life. Be aware of the signs, the feeling of the connection, and where you are led.

If it's in your destiny to further unfold your ability, the process of mentoring offers the student the highest outcomes. With this in mind, it is vitally important for a developing medium to choose wisely when determining who will assist them in the unfoldment and subsequent development of their mediumship.

## Choosing a mentor

So how do you go about acquiring or choosing a mentor? Here's a hint: often it's not about how well-known they are or how high their rates are. It's about the *connection* you make with the mentor, their *track record* in the area you wish to study and their *ability* to communicate with you.

It's my belief that a mentor must resonate with you on an energetic or soul level; there must be a harmonious blending of the energies between you. They must unequivocally and perhaps inexplicably ignite your soul and inspire you to move beyond your limitations and barriers, in both your mediumship and as a person, since the medium and the personality are not easily separated.

Perhaps more importantly, there must be trust between you. You are, after all, putting your mediumship unfoldment and personal development into their hands. They must be ego-less, willing and able to rejoice in your achievements, particularly if at some future time you surpass their own achievements. True Spiritual maturity allows for and even fosters all of this.

Bear in mind that the mentor is trusting that you, too, are willing to rise up to the challenge, to put into practice what you uncover together, and to be humble enough to allow your vulnerability to show. The mentor is asking that you respect them, their experience and their knowledge and that you remain willing to move beyond your comfort zone. That you are self-motivated and disciplined enough to put into practice any suggestions made.

With the acceptance of your trust, your mentor has a responsibility and duty of care towards you as a mentoree, including your wellbeing and your development while you are in their care. In many cases, the mentor may feel they are walking a fine line: push too much and the student tumbles; not enough, and they won't get off the ground.

On a practical level, your mentor must be able to demonstrate mediumship skills in the same areas that you wish to work. For example, if you wish to do public demonstrations, your mentor must have demonstrable skills in this area. They must also be skilled in understanding human nature and most importantly *their own selves*! They must be able to master their own emotions, insecurities, and shadow self and remain open to continuous personal learning. They need to be able to command your respect and have your best interests at heart. They must be savvy enough to discern what your strengths are and able to highlight areas for improvement that are unique to you as a medium. It is not uncommon for the student to eventually become a mentor. If you're interested in becoming a mentor yourself, you'll want your mentor to manifest the qualities within you so that you too can follow that path.

We are all individuals who bring our own special approach to mediumship … and how wonderful it is that this is the case! Just imagine if every medium presented identically – Spirit would not be able to express their uniqueness. If your chosen mentor is trying to turn you into a clone of himself or herself, I would advise that you quickly move on and find another mentor. If this is happening, they do not have your best interests at heart and most likely will have their own vested financial and egoic interests front and center.

Similarly, if a mentor is rigid in their teachings and understanding of mediumship and are themselves unwilling to grow, experiment and learn, then I would also question their suitability to be your mentor. Just imagine a university professor of physics whose mind can't expand with new discoveries about space, quantum fields, time and vibration. Such a person would not be able to meet the needs of his or her students today, and the same is true in the field of mediumship. Just because something has always been done a certain way doesn't mean it must always be done that way. There are many innovations and advancements in our world today and of course this new knowledge now also exists in the world of Spirit.

The veil between the Other Side and physical life is becoming thinner as more and more people accept the reality of life's continuation. Spirit is not a stagnant field of study, but an ever-expanding one! As more and more people of science and technology enter the world of Spirit, they are by default altering the communication process through the knowledge they've accumulated in their earthly lives. It is now not unusual for someone in the Spirit world to make reference to files or photos that are on smartphones by way of proof of survival. This type of evidence would have been inconceivable twenty years ago. Spirit will use whatever tools are available in a given culture to relay their messages in a way that is relevant to the recipients.

There are many well-known mediums who will *certify* you in their style of mediumship – their proven formula, if you like – but for me no one can certify you other than Spirit. Don't give your power away; trust in yourself and trust in your Spirit team. We've now witnessed a high-profile medium and healer renouncing her mediumship, and therefore invalidating her certifications. Don't depend upon written certificates for validation of your talents and experiences; trust yourself and your soul's inner knowing.

Remember, mentoring is a two-way process, requiring responsibility and trust on both sides. It is your job to establish for yourself whether you resonate to your intended mentor's teachings, philosophy, style of teaching, and what they stand for. Once you're secure in your perspective, your mentor will be able to do their job, leading to a successful experience for you both.

## A word to mentors

If you're a mentor of other mediums, you need to have the courage to be honest with your potential student as to whether or not they have what it takes to develop mediumistic ability. Financial gain or other reasons should never enter the equation. Encouraging someone to pursue mediumship who is not wholly suited to it can result in them being distracted from discovering what it is they're truly called to do in this life.

Always make sure students are clear that mediumship doesn't imply they're superior to other people, and that *not* becoming a medium is not a sign of failure, by any means. Every soul has a plan and a purpose; discovering that purpose, whatever it may be, is the greatest joy in life.

On the other hand, if we have a strong intuition about where a mentoree's gifts may lie, we have the unique opportunity and responsibility to advise them to look in that direction.

## My mentor, Mavis Pittilla

The first time I met my mentor, I was feeling like a fish out of water, standing beside a number of excited professional mediums who were using industry jargon that was completely foreign to me. I was in Sydney, Australia attending a five-day residential mediumship course led by her. I felt trepidation and wondered if I'd made the right decision.

Any misgivings immediately dissolved once a seemingly demure, humble and elegant lady who introduced herself as Mavis Pittilla made herself known to me. Hearing her voice and being in her presence left me with a feeling of instant connection and rapport. I felt my heart swell with an instant love for her that typically occurs during a soul-recognition and I immediately felt at ease.

Over the next five days I was mesmerized by her teachings and captivated by her Spirit. She was speaking to my soul and I could feel it expanding and lifting in frequency. She was making so much sense to me, giving me many 'aha' moments. I now had a language and a framework that aligned with my experiences. She contextualized for me all that I had been experiencing up to that point in my life. For the first time in my life I truly understood my nature and myself. I recognized that I was a naturally developed medium.

I was completely self-taught and had no knowledge of the renowned mediums of my day. Although I was working as a professional psychic, I certainly didn't understand the distinction between being psychic and being a medium, and did not even know that I was a true medium!

I left that course with a clear direction and purpose: I knew and understood that I was here to mentor and inspire others as Mavis had me. She became my role model and mentor, and my source of inspiration.

The following year I travelled to England to once again immerse myself in her teachings at the prestigious Arthur Findlay College, the world's foremost college for the advancement of Spiritualism and psychic sciences. During my time with her at the college I was most fortunate to have Mavis officiate during my Spirit naming ceremony, a memory I will treasure forever. In that ceremony, I was told the name that Spirit knows me by and I formally embraced the Spiritualist teachings and philosophy.

What impressed me the most about Mavis were her deep, selfless love, fierce passion and dedication firstly to the Spirit world and then to her students – qualities that I aspire to replicate and continue in my lifetime. I will always be grateful for her and her teachings.

Having stepped into the role of a mentor to many students, I know that the role comes with a great deal of responsibility. Each student I've mentored has left a lasting legacy with me and has taught *me* so much. We truly learn what we teach and teach what we learn. I feel fortunate and grateful to be able to live my purpose and passion and to work with so many beautiful souls.

## Some guidelines for students

As I mentioned, I don't believe you can be *taught* mediumship – you already have the ability within you. What you can be taught, however, is to recognize it, bring awareness to it and to utilize it. In other words, one can be taught the *mechanics* of mediumship.

I believe we all have the ability to be mediums. For some of us, however, it becomes an actual call to service. The old adage 'When the student is ready, the teacher appears' also applies in the field of mediumship. It has certainly been the case for me personally, and I've witnessed the same in my own students. There have been many clients who have said to me that they'd been holding onto my business card for months before finally going ahead and making the booking. Others use phrases like 'I was drawn to you,' 'I felt I had to see you,' or 'I'm not sure *why* I'm here, but I knew I had to be here'. These statements are all examples of the soul rising up to initiate that first step towards walking the life path with purpose.

Here are some general guidelines that will help you get the most out of studying with a mentor:

### Make a commitment

Make a commitment to yourself and to the world of Spirit to maintain continuous learning and to be *responsible* for that learning. The learning doesn't finish at the end of a class or a week's immersion. It's a lifelong commitment; the goal is to evolve as a person, a soul, and a Spirit communicator. It's not just about the time you're committing to your teacher, leader or mentor. You will not grow, expand and progress just by attending a class or reading a book. This is only the start of your education; the rest of it is an inner journey. Books and classes may fill us with enthusiasm, but regular practice and the careful honing of your skills are what result in true excellence. If you're willing to learn, Spirit is more than willing to teach you. Just remember, the commitment to improvement has to start with you, before Spirit can guide you further.

### Respect your mentor and the time they give you

Turn up to your appointments on time, for yourself, for your teacher and for Spirit. Remember, your mentor has invested their time in you and wants to see you become the best you can be. Spirit supports you and has that same wish! You owe it to yourself to be respectful with your time, just as you would for any other meeting that is deeply meaningful in your life.

*Pay attention*
You'll always learn something in your interactions with your mentor. Those small nuggets of wisdom imparted during your time together have the potential to turn into gold when the time is right. Understand that seeds are being planted in your soul that may not yield fruit until later. Your job is to be open to the information offered – just as you want your clients to be when you begin to give readings.

*Know that you will outgrow your mentor*
This is a perfectly natural process, since all fledglings must leave the nest at some point. You'll know when that time is right, and your mentor should be able to confirm this for you.

*Don't put your mentor on a pedestal*
Don't hold your mentor in such esteem that you expect them to be free of flaws or failings; it's very easy to lose sight of the fact that they're human as well. They, like you, have their own set of life circumstances to master, and they deserve the right to make mistakes. If you put your mentor on a pedestal you'll upset the energy dynamic between you, and this will have a detrimental effect on your learning. You'll lose objectivity and the ability to discern for yourself whether what your mentor is saying holds true for you.

*Remember to trust*
One of the biggest hindrances to learning is lack of trust and belief, and the source of this is usually the egoic mind. This lack of confidence doesn't serve you or the Spirit world at all. In order to progress in leaps and bounds, work on building your trust so that you have faith that you've been called to carry out this work.

*Never compare yourself to fellow students*
Remember, your own blueprint is unique and has been designed for the way your soul wishes you to work. Some mediums are born to be

stage performers, filling huge theatres or stadiums, and they have huge personalities that suit that purpose. Other mediums are born to give intimate soul-to-soul readings in a private sitting that bring about deep healing for the recipient. Trust that your work is of equal importance, irrespective of the way that Spirit inspires you and influences your work.

## Stay true to yourself

Stay true to your own unique style of mediumship; be authentic. This point was brought home to me very clearly while I was in Scotland doing a show with two other well-respected mediums. The venue was loud and the attendees were having a wonderful time, enjoying their night out. There was friendly banter and even some good-natured heckling. My two colleagues responded with their own banter and were both very entertaining. They handled the situation well as they're both true professionals, with beautiful strong personalities. My own style of mediumship, however, is very different and if I'd tried to adopt their style it would have come across as awkward and inauthentic. For me, Spirit communication is always about the healing and less about the entertainment. The connections I made for my recipients were reported to me as being heartfelt and healing and those recipients were very grateful for the way I delivered their messages. This reinforced for me again that there is no one way to be a medium, and that I am drawn to the people who resonate with my style.

My final word on being a student … is to always be a student; you're never too young or too old. Keep learning, keep growing and keep evolving. Be open to hearing other points of view, but ultimately trust your own inner authority.

**Exercises**

1.  Watch YouTube videos of mediums you like, to understand their style and way of working.

2.  Ask for recommendations of teachers/mentors and book a time to meet with them to determine if they're a good fit.

3.  Have a reading with your prospective mentor and ask for an assessment of your abilities.

4.  Record yourself working, giving readings, and then critique yourself. Decide which areas you'd like to improve on – public speaking, presentation skills, giving evidence, etc.

5.  Find other non-Spiritual mentors with expertise in the areas you wish to work on; for example, if public speaking is an issue then find a mentor with proven skills and experience in this area.

6.  Practice your skills with other students, particularly if they have a different style to you or are stronger in one of the psychic senses that are underdeveloped in you. Make sure you choose students who are supportive, and remember to back yourself.

7.  Be experimental – try different methods and techniques. Get out of your comfort zone. A development circle is a great place to experiment.

8.  Read widely and become knowledgeable in many fields of interest. Spirit utilizes what you know and will draw upon that information.

CHAPTER 13

# The healing power of mediumship

*'Healing yourself is connected with healing others.'*
*~ Yoko Ono*

Perhaps one of the most significant and yet most overlooked aspects of mediumship is the *healing* that comes about not just for the sitter (the person having the reading), but also for the Spirit person who's connected to the sitter.

As Gordon Higginson wrote in his book *On the Side of Angels,* 'We often forget that Spirit people are subject to difficulties and sometimes need help before they can move forward.' I've witnessed many Spirit people who, knowing they're not wanted at a reading, still make every effort to turn up and apologize for actions, words or outcomes that they were responsible for while living.

Whenever I witness an apology being accepted and see the burden of years of anguish, guilt or shame instantly released, I'm so deeply humbled and moved. Such a release is usually extremely freeing to all involved and is often accompanied by a flood of cleansing tears. Of course, some apologies aren't accepted; the burden of pain carried may be too great to release at that given moment. Even so, I'm grateful that I was able to give that Spirit person a voice and not pass judgment on the nature of the apology.

Healing can also come to sitters who are seeking absolution for a situation for which they cannot forgive themselves – for example, when they didn't make it to the deathbed of their loved one and feel a regret and guilt they're unable to let go. Or they may have argued with their loved one before they passed, leaving healing words unsaid. Or they may have been holding onto an unresolved grievance. There's tremendous relief, healing and letting go once they make contact with their Spirit person and hear the words, 'It's forgiven. I still love you.'

I understand clients who are grappling with such pain, because I've experienced it myself. My maternal grandfather was very ill, and I'd assured him I'd travel to Greece to see him. I'd booked my flight and had my leave approved by my manager at the time, but unfortunately, when it was time for me to fly, my leave approval was revoked. My grandfather passed without seeing me. Needless to say, I was deeply saddened by this and carried anger and remorse about it for years, especially because I'd constantly reassured my grandfather that I was coming to see him. I regretted not fighting for my leave to remain approved, and leaving as planned.

Some time later, when I consulted a medium, my grandfather came through and instantly addressed the guilt I was carrying. He told me that he knew I'd been unable to come to him, so he had come to me! On receiving this message, I was flooded with a memory of an evening when I was startled awake, filled with the knowledge that my grandfather had passed. I sat up and saw him standing at the end of my bed before I fell back to sleep. The following morning my mother telephoned to let me know that he'd passed away.

Being reminded that he'd visited me that night was incredibly healing. I'd been so full of despair that I'd never been able to understand that he had understood my predicament and had come to me instead. At last I was able to let go of the sense that I'd failed him.

In stark contrast, when my grandmother passed, although I was grieving, I was at peace with it. My maternal grandmother was the medium in our family and had a strong sense of knowing. Previously, whenever it was time for me to return to Australia after visiting her, she'd put on the tears and theatrics, claiming she'd die and never see me again. I'd smile and tell her of course she'd see me and wipe her tears away.

The last time I saw her alive, however, was very different. Once again I visited her on the day before my flight back to Australia. This time I sensed a change in my grandmother's behavior and demeanor. She asked me to make her coffee so that we could drink it together. Since my grandmother never drank coffee, this surprised yet delighted me. We were going to share our thoughts as two women over coffee.

After we finished the coffee and I kissed her goodbye, she looked directly into my eyes and said very calmly, 'I will never see you again.' I will never forget that moment as I found myself also having a deep knowing that she was speaking truth. The moment was so potent and a deep understanding was evident between our two souls. We both knew that we were saying goodbye in this physical world.

I returned home to Australia and two months later we received the call that she had passed away. Although I grieved, I was also glad for that one last cup of coffee we'd shared together. Now, of course, I see her daily in the Spirit world as she's taken it upon herself not only to visit me but to assist my students with their development, and she takes great delight in doing this.

The deep healing that occurs when people know that their loved ones are content, that they didn't suffer and that they're still around, humbles me. It can be very distressing and traumatic to see the physical body of our loved ones drawing their final breaths, so to be reassured that their moment of passing was not frightening but a joyous release is such a relief to those left behind. With this knowing, a deep sense of peace filters through into the very core and fiber of their being.

People can be so locked in their grief that they're not able to sleep at night for days, weeks and sometimes months at a time. I've had many people who've had a sitting with me write to say that they've had the best night's sleep in a long time. The confirmation that their loved ones are still around eased the pain of grief, and the connection with them through the power of Spirit made them feel that they were not alone.

Many of us are uncomfortable being around grieving people; the intensity of that emotion can make us feel stressed and helpless. If we are the ones grieving, we may try to hide our feelings and put on a happy face to make others feel better, but suppressed grief will not serve any one in the long run as it can lead to chronic depression and then to a myriad of health issues that result from that depression. It's perfectly natural for us to grieve in a healthy way, feeling our loss and allowing it to flow unbridled.

So how can you help someone who's grieving the loss of a loved one? The answer is to simply be there, fully present, as a witness to their grief. Have you ever noticed that once someone has passed away we start to avoid mentioning him or her, in case we upset the grieving person? We can start to feel awkward and uncomfortable, even inadequate, unsure of how to handle the situation.

I have one very dear friend and cherished client who lost her beloved husband. She revealed to me that a friend had suggested to her that she needed to forget about her loss and get on with life. I'm sure the friend meant well, but for my client this comment cut very deeply; she felt that her many years with her husband were devalued and that he didn't matter anymore. My advice would be to continue to share memories of the departed loved one. It's the greatest gift you can give someone who's grieving, to let them know that their loved one is still valued, cherished and remembered. My client thanked me for talking about her husband and allowing her to share fond memories.

By sharing the memories of our loved ones, we're inviting them to draw near to us and be part of our lives. Some people have said to me that they didn't want to unfairly keep them near if they could be doing other more meaningful things in the world of Spirit, but this is not the case at all. Our departed loved ones cherish being able to spend time with us and being present in our lives. They have the choice and free will do this, so we're not obstructing their Spiritual journey in any way by wanting them to be near us.

Spirit is very intelligent, and at times will bring particular songs forward as a means of communicating to bring about healing. I recall sitting for a family once who had lost their son and brother. The young man in Spirit (I'll call him Tim) was a musician and was writing a wedding song for his sister but did not get to complete it. He told me that the song and its lyrics were in a black notebook that was now with his brother. As the reading progressed, Tim asked his brother – who was also a musician – to finish the song off for him. You can imagine his brother's look of stunned amazement when I passed on this information. That completed song provided much healing for this grieving family. I sat for the family again some time later and they confirmed that the song was played at his sister's wedding. It was such a special, poignant moment for everyone involved, and gave them irrefutable confirmation that their beloved Tim was with them in Spirit.

Spirit will also be motivated to provide healing from the other side to their own family members and will use whatever means they can to bring this about, especially at times of great importance; they will move heaven and earth to bring about their desires. I witnessed this in the most profound and humbling way at the funeral of a dear friend of mine. My beautiful friend had been diagnosed with a brain tumor that unfortunately was terminal; she was a single mum to a daughter who was the same age as mine. As her illness progressed she said a couple of things to me that will remain forever in my heart.

She had come to terms with her fate and I recall her looking directly into my eyes and touching my soul as she informed me that her last job on earth would be the best one of all. Knowing that she was unable to work due to her illness, I asked her what that job was.

She replied, 'I get to be love. My last job is to radiate unconditional love to all those I come into contact with, and that's the best job of all.' I found myself shaking from head to toe as the profoundness of what she'd said sank into me.

Just prior to her passing she held my hand and told me, with her trademark sense of humor, that after she died she'd come back and haunt me. True to her word, she did just that! On the morning of her passing, I woke to find her Spirit standing at the foot of my bed. She smiled at me and told me she was at peace now and that she wanted me to look after her daughter at her funeral. I reassured her that I would, but on the day of her funeral, even though I'd arrived early, I found the church overflowing with people who had spilled out onto the street. I felt dismayed, wondering how I was even going to make my way into the church through the crowd. I'd managed to get into the foyer when all of a sudden an usher tapped me on the shoulder and directed me into the church, letting me know that there was a spare seat at the front of the church along the wall.

When I sat down in the seat he'd directed me to I was stunned to see that I was sitting directly facing my friend's daughter. I smiled and sent her a silent thank you and knew she'd orchestrated this; she was one determined lady. I sat quietly and sent her daughter reiki healing and support throughout the service, in particular when she was giving her eulogy. I could see her falter; she really wanted to speak but at the same time she felt overwhelmed by the enormity of the day. I feel that the energetic support she received from me got her over the line.

There are many stories of healing I could share but the common denominator is that there's a tremendous sense of peace when sitters have understood that life is eternal, that love lives on and that our loved ones are never lost to us.

This healing chapter is perhaps one of the most important for me, as it highlights why I've agreed to work with Spirit on a daily basis. It's deeply moving for me to witness the deep healing that a mediumship session can deliver to those who are suffering in their loss and grief.

The transformation that comes from being able to move on with life a little lighter, knowing that your loved ones beyond the veil are well, happy and very much a part of your life, is incredibly life-changing.

CHAPTER 14

# Nurturing the young medium

*'What is love? It's a party in your heart.'*
*~ My daughter, age 4*

Mediums are born; you cannot be *taught* to be a medium. They come into this world with their ability firmly in place. Even if they have no awareness of this ability it is ingrained as part of their soul's unique expression in this lifetime. At birth, their soul is fully equipped to unfold their mediumship at a predefined moment in their lives.

Those who are born with this ability commonly show traits in early childhood. It is not uncommon for parents to find their infant is smiling into empty space as if they were watching another person. Many parents report that by the time that their child is able to speak they are having conversations with *imaginary* friends.

Should this mediumship ability be stimulated in a very young person, it will usually fade during their formative years, as was the case with me. This is so that the developing child can become grounded and live securely in the physical world. When the child has grown beyond the formative years (during which the balance of physical and Spiritual life is established), the ability usually appears again.

One thing I know from personal experience is that Spirit loves children! I recall many a night going into the nursery to feed my baby only to find the room filled with people in Spirit oohing and aahing at my baby girl, waking her up at 3 in the morning! At times I'd also hear her laughing in her cot as if her grandfather in Spirit was playing with her. One particular night when she was just eight weeks old and wrapped in a swaddling blanket I noticed that a huge teddy bear that sat at the top end of the cot was lying down by her feet, as if someone had dropped it in a hurry. She also had a baby gym play mat that she lay under that played a song when she kicked a particular spot. There were many nights that I heard the mat play music after we'd all gone to sleep.

Each medium's blossoming is unique to their own journey; however, there are traits and characteristics that are hallmarks of a junior medium. It is these traits that I wish to explore further in this section. Know that this list is not exhaustive but is based on my personal experience and my experience as a mentor of other mediums.

## Characteristics of a young medium

*Ultrasensitive*

In many cultures, sensitivity is considered a weakness or a negative character trait – something to get over, something that needs fixing. But from a young medium's perspective, being overly sensitive is a *must,* since it's part of the tool kit they're developing, and will serve them well in years to come.

It is through the filter of the central nervous system that all subtle information comes from Spirit. It's then processed and has meaning assigned to it. A medium's nervous system is effectively their main *tool of the trade*. One of the challenges for children who are natural mediums is that they can become overwhelmed with sensory stimulation. This means they're flooded with people's thoughts and feelings while simultaneously trying to understand their own feelings, emotions and thoughts and how they work.

They enter nursery schools or classrooms and their behavior changes drastically, often contributing to their mother's guilt. In a controlled environment, such as their home, their behavior is great, but when placed elsewhere, they suddenly have outbursts or tantrums. If they're lucky, they'll have one in-tune parent who can guide them safely through these early developmental days. Most of us, however, were born into families where this was not the case. We had to navigate our life without this guidance, trying to work out what was going on. It's important that we don't hold onto feelings of resentment towards our parents, who did not understand us as children.

As a child I was often labeled highly strung, as having a nervous disposition, as anxious and sensitive. I have early memories of always being at the doctor with a sore tummy. This usually happened when I was placed in situations that I wasn't comfortable in, like joining a new school, or having to stand up in front of the class, or being unfamiliar with a topic or activity. All these situations could trigger reactions in my nervous system. I now realize that most of what I was feeling was not even mine – I was absorbing the thoughts and feelings of those around me due to my highly *empathic nature*.

I now understand my childhood and have been able to reframe my past as a positive experience. Where I once believed what the doctors and others were telling me regarding my sensitivity, I now realize that I was taking on the energy of others and was unable to process that energy.

One of the ways that my own Spirit guides taught me to close off my sensitivity was to first discern which energies were mine and which I'd absorbed from others. For example, if I suddenly developed anxiety when previously I was perfectly fine, I'd state in my mind, 'If this anxiety is not mine – please take it away.' If the anxiety left, that confirmed that I had in fact picked up anxiety from someone around me. This was very affirming for me and I learnt where the boundary that defined me started and ended.

The process of becoming grounded was fundamental to the mastery of my sensitivity. I utilized a technique whereby I visualized ruby red shafts of light moving through each of my legs and being embedded into the core of Mother Earth. I'd experience an immediate sense of inner strength and security. By being grounded I was more strongly anchored within myself and less likely to take on the thoughts and feelings of others. Mastering these techniques and others allowed me to clearly define who I was and to claim space for myself.

Being empathic is a tool that serves all mediums when it is understood and used efficiently. Young mediums must learn about their empathic nature and how to navigate life without becoming overwhelmed. They must learn about boundaries so they can discern where they end and others begin. Recognizing that many of their feelings and moods are not their own is an important part of their soul's education. If you're a parent or caretaker of an empathic child, you have the rare opportunity to be an anchor for them – a constant in a world where the energies they sense shift and change. Try to remain mindful of the fact that you've been placed in their lives to support them as they struggle to learn how to balance the world of Spirit with their physical surroundings.

It's essential to teach them basic life skills that will serve them well later in life, particularly if they choose to be of service to the Spirit world. These skills include such things as knowing what to do to increase their sense of being *grounded*. These children thrive in being outside in nature, preferably barefoot, so that they make contact with the Earth. When their feet touch the ground, a circuit is created via which they can transfer the excess energies they've absorbed into their auric field safely into the Earth. By relieving themselves of this excess energy, they're able to calm the nervous system and be free of the emotional interferences that distract them from their own feelings and thoughts. They can then focus on understanding and expressing their true selves, confident in their thoughts, their feelings and their sense of individuality.

If left ungrounded, empathic children may become hypersensitive, presenting with various psychosomatic concerns such as inexplicable stomach pains and nausea, headaches and fatigue. Since they find it difficult to relax and switch off, they may isolate themselves as a means of coping, or act out, flying into rages or fits of crying. Sensitive children often reflect issues that are unacknowledged or unspoken in the people around them. As empaths, they seek to heal family dynamics by bringing to light the repressed emotions that their parents or other family members are grappling with. Whenever you observe a young medium absorbing, manifesting or talking about the anger, depression or sadness of others, remember that they are trying to subconsciously heal and neutralize toxic emotions.

Listening with openness and reflecting back what an empathetic child is feeling can be immensely helpful to them. By validating their feelings you give them the confidence to trust their own perceptions. For example, if they don't want to kiss a relative hello, then honor their feelings and don't insist on it. They're tuning in to their own perceptions, and it's important that they receive the support and validation they require while they're fine-tuning their skills.

I recall that my daughter at around the age of four would look at people in the shops and turn to me and say in a loud voice, 'Mummy, we don't like her!' What she was doing was feeling the person's auric field and deciding it was not harmonious for her. I let her know that I understood her meaning, keeping it simple and used her language to verify her feelings. Conversely, when she saw someone she instantly resonated with, she would say, 'Mummy, I like her!' This was her way of becoming familiar with the energies she liked and felt comfortable with versus those that she did not.

Of course, there are times that a child might actually have a medical issue or a condition such as autism, schizophrenia or Asperger's, to name but a few. I always encourage a parent to seek a medical opinion to be reassured if they have any doubts as to the source of the child's behavior.

### Being overly helpful

From a very early age you'll find young mediums being helpful, even when help is neither required nor wanted. It's inherent in their soul's make-up. Later in life they may express this deep, innate desire to help through giving readings or healings to others. What you can do to nurture and develop this desire within them is to teach them healthy ways of helping. They must first understand that they need to be asked to help, or that they must ask first if they might be of help, before jumping in to do so.

Healthy boundaries set up now will stand them in good stead, so that they don't get burnt-out in the future and don't feel unappreciated or undervalued. It's vitally important that they learn as early as possible that it is acceptable to help others, providing it's not at the cost of their own health and wellbeing. A medium must continuously balance how often they open their nervous system to be used by Spirit with how often they need to replenish their own energy stores so they do not become depleted. Awareness of this begins in childhood.

### Imaginary friends

Young mediums are the ones with *real* imaginary friends. These friends are described in vivid detail, including name, age and what they're wearing. Long conversations are held, and the body language of the child suggests that another person is present. Through my work as a professional medium, I've heard countless stories of the children of my clients and students being observed speaking to people who were unseen. These friends were not just restricted to *people* in Spirit; there are cases where children describe animals from the world of Spirit.

The first time I saw my daughter speaking to Spirit was when she was sitting on the toilet, of all things! She was almost three when I overheard her saying, 'Hey, stop following me into the toilet.' Since we were the only two physical people in the house at that time, I asked her who she was speaking to. She replied, 'I'm talking to the man.' Initially, my heart was pounding. I then asked her if he was a nice man and what his name was. She replied, 'It's Papou', which means 'grandfather' in Greek. I then asked her what he was doing and she replied that he was tickling her on her tummy.

In this instance, her paternal grandfather – who'd passed many years ago, before I'd met my husband – was communicating and playing with my daughter. I'd never shown her a photo of him and because I'd never met him, I had no stories to share about him. Following that encounter I showed her a photo of her grandfather and asked her who it was; she relied instantly, 'Papou' – a great confirmation.

If your child is talking to you about imaginary friends, resist the temptation to dismiss this as a vivid imagination. Be open to the possibility that they may in fact be communicating with Spirit; you can be assured that they're safe. It's most likely the loved ones that they're communicating with are their grandparents or other family members. Be open and curious. Ask your child questions about their friends in a casual way. Ask them about identifiers such as names and what they're wearing and then expand to include what they're saying and doing. Teach your child to trust what they're seeing and to be feel confident to share it with you.

Most importantly, remember to allow your child to be a child as well. Don't build your child up to be something they may not actually be. Many parents have a desire for their child to be considered special or unique. Be objective, and careful not to project personal desires onto them. They're children first and foremost, and they deserve to have their own childhood, just as you had yours.

If they're approaching you and asking questions, certainly acknowledge and validate them. This is how they learn to trust their psychic perceptions and what they're feeling. If they're not approaching you about such subjects, then let them simply enjoy their childhood without being questioned or made to perform.

## Curiosity

All mediums are born with an innate curiosity – quite frankly, they're nosy! They'll often be told to mind their own business, but for them this is an impossible task. Their minds are always tuning in to *the story behind the story*. They want to find out how things work and, most of all, what makes people tick. They're deeply aware that things are not always what they appear to be at first glance, so they tend to ask a lot of questions.

It's precisely this natural interest in the ways of human thinking and behavior that will make them excellent evidential mediums. They effectively become a *This Is Your Life* reporter, bringing forward evidence of achievements, relationships, personal history and other verifiable facts from their contacts in the Spirit world!

For me, when I invite Spirit to make a connection with me, I'm inviting a most honored and sacred guest to enter my home, to sit and chat with me. I become interested in my guest and ask about them. It's important to request information with respect and reverence and not to simply interrogate the Spirit person. Demanding answers that could make me look great as a medium might not actually be showing respect to the Spirit person, their time, or their unique perspective. Here's where the previously mentioned three Rs of mediumship – *respect, reverence and responsibility* – are important. I consider them to be priorities in my work.

## Highly creative

All children are creative to some degree, but with young mediums you'll find this natural creativity is evident from a very early age. They may be natural performers, musicians, actors or artists, or they might express their creativity in a more hands-on way. What's happening, in essence, is that they're tapping into the universal stream of creation and acting as a conduit for ideas. You might think of this stream as a kind of Spiritual internet, where one accesses whatever information is needed at a given time.

From very early in our school years we're encouraged to exercise our logical mind, which is full of facts, figures, reasoning and deduction, leaving the right side of the brain underutilized. It is very advantageous to encourage in our young mediums – without pressure – this natural creativity, and to support their creative pursuits as long as possible throughout their schooling. Creative pursuits strengthen the right side of the brain, which is the part that allows us to access our intuition. Even if children don't have psychic talents, providing opportunities for creative expression is extremely beneficial to their mental, emotional and physical health. It's commonly agreed among educators today that creative outlets enhance intelligence in people of all ages.

Spirit communicated to me some time ago that the next evolution of humans would be *whole brain integrated thinkers* rather than right- or left-brain thinkers. We're seeing more and more sensitive children not being able to cope with mainstream teaching environments that cater predominantly for the left-brain thinker. At present, left-brain thinkers are valued for their business and practical acumen and ability to make money, while right-brain thinkers are often considered unworthy of equal compensation. It's my hope that a social model based on educating the whole brain will eventually change humanity's view of the value of creative people, Spiritual teachers and healers, ushering in an age of true equality and a more balanced approach to caring for one's whole being. With this in mind, we as parents and guardians can look for schools for our children that have a more creative focus. If this isn't possible, find a way to introduce opportunities for creativity at home or through after-school programs.

I recall as a child making up plays and scenarios and acting them out with my brothers. My favorite pastimes were drawing, coloring-in, and reading alone. It may sound boring, but my inner world was rich with imagination as I poured into my playtime a plethora of exciting plots, places, characters, and more. I see now that these seemingly innocent childhood activities were essentially training practices, leading me to my vocation as a professional medium. By exercising my intuitive side as a child, I was better prepared as an adult to draw upon these inner resources when making contacts with Spirit.

Volumes have been written about how children of the internet generation have not had the opportunity to explore their imaginations the way the generations before them did. Before our lives were so technology-driven, children played outdoors most of the time and spent hours making things out of common objects, acting out scenarios, and exploring the world without constant parental supervision or direction. Children learned to solve problems, be independent, follow their creative urges, and to fill their time with the fruits of their imagination rather than relying on TV and computers to supply them with entertainment. I say this with the understanding that we can't turn back time and that there are many merits to technology; however, the sensitive child needs much more freedom to live in their imagination than most, and we may find we have to deliberately create the experience of freedom for them.

*Feeling alone*

Young mediums may feel alone or different to other children. They often populate the fringe groups in social circles and although they desperately want to belong, feel disconnected in some way. They recognize at a deep level that they're different, but they don't have the words to define this difference or the life experience to understand it. They have an internal radar system when determining who is like them, and they'll often gravitate towards other children who appear to be misfits as well. These children are desperately seeking validation and acceptance – a basic human right for us all but one that is not naturally afforded to them. Paradoxically, they're also fiercely independent, and often difficult to parent due to their willful natures. They march to the beat of their own drum and will not be easily influenced or swayed.

The living and schooling experiences of young mediums may also make them feel alone. In my case, my parents moved every two or three years, so I was forever the new child at school. Since I was never around long enough to form lifelong friends, I had to rely on my inner life for fulfillment. Being alone so much also taught me resilience, adaptability and self-reliance. I developed the ability to quickly read people and environments and to respond accordingly – a skill that continues to be helpful in my life.

### Natural healers

Being highly empathic in nature, young mediums are natural healers. They'll listen intently to their friend's woes and offer words of wisdom that are beyond their physical years. They will want to care for their animals if they are unwell and will intuitively know what do.

They are the first to rush in and offer a sympathetic hug. I recall my daughter at age one running away from me at a coffee shop towards a very elderly gentleman sitting at another table with his wife. My daughter spontaneously threw her arms around his neck and gave him a huge kiss on the cheek. Of course I was mortified and quickly went over to retrieve my child, apologizing for her intrusion. The gentleman in question burst into tears, and his wife said, with tears in her eyes, 'Please don't apologize. He so needed that kiss today.' This was a beautiful example and a reminder to me that we never know when a natural healer (in this case my daughter) will be called upon by Spirit to reach out to someone to supply physical, emotional or mental healing.

In other instances you may overhear your children talking to their healing angels or guides. Take an interest in their conversations and gently ask questions, taking your cues from the child as to how much they want to divulge. Find out what their healing guides are here to help with and the methods they're using to work with your child. You may notice that your child instinctively wants to place their hands on others to take away the hurt. Although this is a beautiful thing to do, remind them to always ask permission from the other person and to look after themselves before they assist others. Professional healers learn to open a healing session and close it so that their own energy stays intact. It may be helpful with a young medium to guide them to create a simple form of opening and closing themselves. In my reiki classes, I teach my younger students to say, with concentrated intention, 'Healing on' and 'Healing off', to begin and close their practice. This will prevent them from feeling overwhelmed or developing burnout and will establish healthy boundaries that will become especially useful as they mature.

Other children will use laughter, the highest form of healing, to heal those around them. The class clown may in fact be a natural healer in disguise, responding to the undercurrents in the classroom. Laughter truly *is* the best medicine, for it literally fills the body with endorphins, which activate healing automatically. An American physician, Norman Cousins, in his book *Anatomy of an Illness*, describes how he filled his hospital room with comedic friends and insisted on watching hilarious movies non-stop during his illness. After experiencing a bout of laughter, he'd measure the sedimentary rate of his blood. Through this experiment, he was able to scientifically prove that laughter improved the results. He recovered from his illness, astounding the medical profession, and became a lifelong proponent of joy as a healing agent in life. Many young mediums manifest this wisdom, reminding us to have a light and happy heart as we work with Spirit.

### An affinity for crystals

Young mediums often gravitate towards crystals and other stones and jewels, sensing in them their inherent healing power. Most parents will report that their sensitive children's eyes light up as if they're in a candy store when they come across crystals. As they grow and mature they may also choose to wear crystal jewelry, and this applies to both genders. By the time they hit their teens, they've usually amassed a vast collection of these energetically charged stones.

Oftentimes, these young ones will initiate magical activities with their crystals. For example, they may intuitively hold a crystal to a part of their body or the bodies of others in an attempt to facilitate healing. They may not be able to find adequate words to explain their actions, but somehow they know how to choose the correct crystals according to what the body needs at a given time. I've personally witnessed children using crystal grids to heal family members or friends. The gridding process is something they intuitively know how to do without having received any instruction or training; their knowledge comes from an inner source.

## Animal lovers

These highly sensitive children usually have a great empathy and affinity for animals, and this is usually demonstrated at a very young age. They're naturally drawn to the animal kingdom and will personify their pets, treating them as people. They are usually an advocate for animal rights and will often bring stray animals home to protect, nurture and look after them. They may also gravitate naturally to vegetarianism. Such experiences can be troubling for children, for they may tune in to the suffering of animals to an extreme degree, and yearn to alleviate it. This is where we as adults can help our young ones navigate the subject of compassion, teaching them that while they're but one person and not responsible for everything, they can certainly do their share and through example inspire others to do the same. On the other hand, this special connection to animals can also bring them great happiness. You may observe them spending long periods of time watching animals in their natural setting. Whenever possible, it is wise to give them the chance to bask in the healing energy of Nature, for they find tremendous comfort there.

As a child, I was forever convincing my parents to house yet another stray cat or dog. At one stage I'd accumulated one orphan horse, two orphan lambs, five stray cats, two dogs and a parrot! Because they identify with all animals, these children may have unusual or non-typical pets in addition to stray cats or dogs. In our case, my daughter currently has an Australian bearded dragon lizard named Spike whom she adores. I must admit he's grown on me too!

Mediumistic children will often be naturals at animal communication. This, in my opinion, is achieved via telepathic connection, the direct linking of thoughts. I recall taking my daughter to visit horses on a farm and teaching her to refine this skill set further. I'd ask her to call the horses over not with her voice but with her heart and mind. Without fail, the horses always lifted their heads to look at us briefly before making their way over. In sharp contrast, we'd observe other children calling out to the horses, only to be ignored completely as the horses carried on grazing in the paddocks.

I too have had many telepathic experiences with animals but the most profound one for me was an encounter I had swimming with wild dolphins in Hawaii. I was on a boat with many others seeking this experience and we were informed that if a dolphin shows its underbelly to you, it's a sign of affection and trust. After jumping in the water I had an urge to move away from the main group of swimmers. Floating, I looked down into the depths and saw a pod of dolphins swim under my body. One dolphin in particular stayed beneath me and turned to show me its belly. We made direct eye contact and I heard telepathically the words 'I see you.' With great delight I beamed back 'I see YOU' and was overcome with great joy and love. The dolphin sent sonar waves into my heart center and then waved its flipper before swimming on to join its family. I was generously given an incredible gift of connection by that amazing dolphin.

*Environmentally aware*

Such deep love for Nature fosters in such children a corresponding passion for preserving and healing the entire natural world. You may witness your sensitive child becoming emotional over such subjects as pollution, extinction of plants and animals, global warming and similar issues. Their feelings are strong and authentic, and it's important to take them seriously, not only out of respect for them but because these issues are pressing for every Spiritually aware person today.

There's a wave of consciousness sweeping the planet designed to stir humanity to change their thinking patterns, and in turn their behavior, regarding the care of Mother Earth. These children are part of that wave, and have much to teach us older ones about how to live. Young mediums are specially equipped to learn, lead, and teach about the various social and environmental issues that humanity faces today. As their caretakers, we must remember they are vulnerable to their feelings about the world's suffering. It's truly a privilege and an honor to be in a position to help them learn to balance their thoughts and emotions regarding the Earth and her inhabitants. In addition, let's not forget that these souls in young bodies are our teachers as well. If we open our hearts to them and strive to see through their eyes, we can learn to see the wonders of life with more gratitude, to feel each moment more authentically, to love the earth more deeply, and to relax into the present moment more fully.

Sensitivity to the world of Nature can be observed at an extremely young age in such children. They take great delight in observing and interacting with plants and creatures, both great and small. Instinctively they know that the wellbeing of all life forms is interconnected, and that what they give to the natural world they also receive. They understand that to harm Nature is to harm oneself, and recognize that pollution adds stress not only to animals and plants but to their own lives as well. When they pet an animal or express love to a plant, they find that they are also soothed and healed at the soul level.

So often in today's rush, we forget to give our sensitive children the time they need to smell the roses, to dream and reflect, to simply *be* in an unstructured manner. Meeting the young medium's needs may require that we slow down a bit ourselves, so that we're not hurrying them from one activity to another without some pockets of quiet time in between. I have fond memories of my daughter in her preschool years singing to the trees at the end of our driveway before she got into the car each morning. She would absolutely refuse to get into the car until she'd finished letting the trees know how much she loved them. Knowing that they felt loved gave her a sense of deep contentment and put her into the right frame of mind to begin her day. Once I recognized this, I began to allot extra time each morning so she could perform her loving ritual with the trees. If you find your child needing to connect with Nature in order to get into a mindset of peace and happiness, I advise you to patiently support their impulse to do so and allow extra time for it to happen.

## General guidelines

I've described here a variety of ways to support and nurture the young medium, but each is also appropriate for children in general. In other words, these are sound and stable ways of raising any child to be a balanced, caring individual. It's important to remember that while we want to make space for a child's intuition to develop, we don't want to push them or project onto them our own desires. Nor is it wise to hurry a child to open their mediumship abilities. There's no need to identify or label your child as a medium, or to make them feel special; *all* children are special. It's good, though, if your child is asking questions or expressing curiosity, to normalize the conversation and answer to the best of your ability.

It's important that as a parent you don't allow your own fears and insecurities to overshadow your child. Fear is only present when there's a lack of understanding, so it's a good idea to learn as much about the topic as possible so that you can guide your young charge with wisdom. Bear in mind, too, that each person's relationship with Spirit is unique and intimate. We need to respect one another's methods of contact and interpretation, and this is true for children as well as adults. Avoid molding your child's approach to Spirit after your own ways. They have a destiny of their own, just as we do, and we're there to love, observe, and respond to teachable moments, not to control them or to force on them our opinions and ideas.

It's my belief that Spirit will not harm a child, since the impulse of Spirit is always to love, guide, and enlighten. When things go bump in the night it may be Spirit's way of trying to communicate and get your child's attention – or it may be your child's vivid imagination. The main objective is to equip your child with the confidence to discern for themselves whether it's Spirit or their mind giving in to fearful thoughts.

If your child is being woken at night, it's important to teach your child about boundaries and what's appropriate versus what is not. They have full control over how Spirit interacts with them, and when. Teach your child to ask Spirit not to wake or interrupt them at night. You can explain to them that working with the Spirit world is exactly the same as working with the physical world. You wouldn't allow an adult to wake your child at night when they're sleeping, and the same applies to Spirit. Help your child to see that their relationship with Spirit is not a passive one. Rather, they become empowered when they direct Spirit and teach them when it's appropriate for them to be in contact.

All children are entitled to have *a party in their hearts*. If these experiences aren't comfortable and meaningful for your child and they're frequently telling you that they feel afraid, let them know that you take them seriously. Never scoff at or dismiss a child's experiences; rather, listen as long as they need to talk without interrupting or correcting. Let their questions be your guide as to how much to explain to them, and if you aren't certain of the answer, say so and assure them that you'll find out from someone who knows. The goal is to help them develop a skill set they can use to cope with the experiences they're having. Do they need to go out in the sunshine, play a game, read or draw to redirect their energy for a while, and to soothe the tension they're feeling? Do they need an explanation for the things they sense, or a special night-time ritual to reassure them?

I've worked with quite a few young mediums and explained to them that they're allowed to choose when they want to connect with Spirit, encouraging them to pick a time when they'll give Spirit their attention and tell Spirit to only come at that time. One child told me she wanted the Spirits to meet her at a tree outside, not to come into the house, and I guided her into setting those boundaries up with Spirit. In this way, she felt she was meeting them on her terms. Other children may wonder exactly what Spirit is and isn't. Oftentimes, the simple explanation that they're a type of angel who wants to check on them and protect them may suffice. The idea is for the mediumship abilities of children to become a natural part of their life, not to dominate their thoughts, so that they have the time they need to grow up and develop essential, practical life skills.

Above all, be totally honest and never lie to them. If, for example, they say to you 'I think you're sad in your heart' and this is true, don't pretend that you're not. Acknowledge the feeling in simple, understandable words so that they can learn to trust in their perceptions and abilities. There will be times that we'll wonder if we're doing and saying the right thing with our sensitive child, but this is true of any parent of any child. Let us strive to do our best without giving in to too much guilt or self-doubt, remembering that although we are not perfect parents, we *are* the right parent for our child ... for they chose us.

**Exercises**

1. Ask your child to visualize a golden bubble or balloon and then to imagine that the balloon completely surrounds them. Have them say aloud, 'I am in my bubble 100 per cent of the time.' This allows your child to limit their exposure to other people's energies so they can learn to discern what is their energy versus what they're absorbing from everyone else.

2. To help them understand what they've taken on energetically, ask them to identify a feeling or physical symptom, such as anger or a headache, and then to ask aloud, 'If this (insert symptom or feeling here) is not mine, then please take it away.' If the feeling or symptom goes, they can know that they've empathetically picked up someone else's energies. This helps them work out where their own auric field starts and finishes.

3. To facilitate grounding, have them pretend that they're a tree. Ask them to imagine that they're growing tree roots from the bottoms of their feet and that those roots are making their way deep into Mother Earth. Ask them to stand tall and strong, thinking of their torso as the tree trunk. Then tell them to imagine that the strands of their hair are the branches and leaves reaching up to the sun, absorbing the golden rays into their head.

4. If your child has made you aware that they're actually seeing Spirit, then coach them to have direct conversations with Spirit. Discuss what they want to say to Spirit and if they need help with the words, assist them in finding the right ones. Coach your child on how to set up boundaries around when they wish to communicate with Spirit and when they do not. By normalizing and validating the idea of conversing with Spirit, you'll help your child become more comfortable with their experiences.

5. Introduce your child to simple tools such as oracle cards and crystals to help them direct their energies and thoughts. Without pressuring them, show them how to shuffle and select a card whenever they feel the need. Ask them what they think the card means, what special message it has for them. Make this a game. In my opinion, it's best to let children use their intuition rather than relying on the card's booklet for an explanation. Ask them what jumps out at them as they look at the card – a certain color, word, picture, or general feeling? Be careful not to put words in their mouths or push them into a certain interpretation. Listen, accept, and reflect what they say and how they feel. In choosing crystals, allow them to select the ones they're drawn to and encourage them to hold or arrange their crystals whenever they wish. You may find that just as some children choose certain toys to cuddle or play with when they're stressed, your young medium will use these crystals and cards to refocus, relax, or gain clarity. Cards that I like for children are Creature Teacher by Scott Alexander King or The Magical Unicorns by Doreen Virtue.

6. Enroll your child in activities that strengthen their energy, such as karate, tai chi or yoga. The beauty of these activities is that they help children learn how to combine and focus their physical, mental and Spiritual energy in a positive and healthy way.

7. Nurture your child's creative side as much as possible through participation in activities such as art, dance, music, drama, cooking, gardening, construction and more. Most of the time, children will let you know which creative area appeals to them. Nurturing creativity activates the right side of the brain. Again, be sure to protect your child's free time so that they don't become overscheduled.

8. Encourage your child to communicate with family pets and other animals, acknowledging the fact that animals have

emotions that are expressed telepathically through images and physical cues. Suggest that they experiment with sending an animal a mental image of a direction – for example, sitting on their mat – and then observe how the animal responds. Encourage them to simply listen to the animal's energy to see if they can pick up the image or emotion the animal is directing towards them

# Coda – and an invitation

I've written this book to inspire you to trust in yourself, to believe in your ability and to invite you to welcome Spirit into your hearts and home. If after reading this book you feel motivated to be an ambassador for Spirit – to give Spirit a voice – then I strongly encourage you to continue with your practice and with your development. Let Spirit move and inspire you on a daily basis; ask them to show you the way, to illuminate your path.

Allow yourself to develop at your own rate, without feeling inadequate or comparing yourself to others. If you know that this is your calling and you cannot imagine yourself doing anything else in life, then know in your heart that you'll be well supported by the Spirit world as they rejoice in the fact that you've joined their team.

If you need support and encouragement then please become part of my online community by joining me on my Facebook page, www.facebook.com/IoannaSerpanos, or reach out on my website: www.ioannaserpanos.com. I look forward to hearing how Spirit has uplifted your life and motivated you in your practice, and to sharing in and reading your stories. This is not the end; rather it's your beginning and I am so excited for you.

# Acknowledgements

There are many people, in spirit and in person that I would like to acknowledge.

To Sandra Nehmet who predicted in 1987 that I would write this book. Your prediction has just come true.

To all past and current students and clients, thank you for the opportunity to work with you and to learn from you. You have all touched my heart in ways that you will never know. You have shared your lives, your hopes, your dreams and your sorrows with me. I have laughed with you and I have cried with you and I have been both humbled and blessed by the experience.

This book would still be sitting in my computer if it wasn't for the assistance and help of my editors. To my amazing content editor Frances Key whom I now consider a soul sister and dear friend. Our chats and insights have been soul balm for me. Tricia Dearborn, thank you for polishing my manuscript and refining my content and meaning. Your professionalism is second to none.

Being supported whist writing, operating my business and being mum would be impossible without a supportive team behind me. To my amazing, loyal and inspiring assistants and friends, Nicky Ellis, Emma Coates and Michelle Goodier, I thank you. Words are not enough.

To those I haven't acknowledged specifically, know that I carry you all in my heart. Especially my tribe of loyal and supportive friends for allowing me to bounce ideas, to dream, to plan and to hope, knowing that you love me exactly as I am.

Finally, to my beloved mother Christina, for your constant unwavering support and love and your genetics that carry our gift. To my father Nicholas for motivating me to succeed, to strive and to always turn up.

Of course my acknowledgements would not be complete without expressing my deepest gratitude to my maternal grandmother, Efstatheia, who takes great delight in helping my students develop their ability from the other side. I couldn't live without your love, support and friendship - simply, thank you.

# ABOUT THE AUTHOR

Ioanna Serpanos is a renowned medium, psychic and mentor. Known for her heartfelt authenticity, she believes mediumship is a vehicle for healing. She has touched hundreds of lives with her unique ability to connect loved ones on the other side.

A passionate educator, Ioanna regularly runs seminars and workshops highlighting the principals of strong mediumship. A qualified engineer, she marries sound practical techniques with her esoteric and spiritual teachings.

She is a mother, an avid reader and traveller and lives in Melbourne, Australia.

CPSIA information can be obtained
at www.ICGtesting.com
Printed in the USA
LVHW05075030623
751144LV00032B/945/J

9 780648 525004